PRAISE FOR *CHASING SOCIAL JUSTICE*

"Laurie Sherman has a special gift for weaving together how the personal is political, demonstrating how the work of creating a socially just world is inextricably linked with acknowledging the humanity in each person and the connections between us. As someone who focuses on structural change, I deeply appreciate the way she draws us in with stories that open our hearts, and then draws out the lessons from each one."

BRIAN CORR, NATIONAL ASSOCIATION FOR CIVILIAN OVERSIGHT OF LAW ENFORCEMENT, MASSACHUSETTS DEMOCRATIC STATE COMMITTEE

"This is just what we need to get ready for the next battle in the never-ending effort to make this a better world. And it comes at just the right time."

MICHAEL DUKAKIS, FORMER GOVERNOR OF MASSACHUSETTS, PRESIDENTIAL NOMINFF, DISTINGUISHED PROFESSOR OF POLITICAL SCIENCE AT NORTHEASTERN UNIVERSITY

"Born out of her years of experience in non-profits, city government, local politics, and a personal quest to leave the world better than she found it, Sherman offers readers an antidote for the uncertainty about what we can do in the face of intolerance and inequities. Each chapter offers practical advice and strategies. The book concludes with discussion questions to stimulate dialogue and action. What a great tool to 'get smart' about building a better neighborhood, city, and world."

DEBORAH J. HIRSCH, PRESIDENT, WOODROW WILSON GRADUATE SCHOOL OF TEACHING AND LEARNING

"In *Chasing Social Justice* Laurie Sherman brings a lifetime of insights about how change happens, and how we can all do more to ask better questions, build bigger coalitions, and tell more powerful stories – in service of a fairer world. This is a great book. I encourage you to read it, discuss it and pass it on!"

ERIC SCHWARZ, AUTHOR OF *THE OPPORTUNITY EQUATION*, CEO OF COLLEGE FOR SOCIAL INNOVATION, CO-FOUNDER OF CITIZEN SCHOOLS

"We in the United States must become the Ancestors future generations look to with pride. Here, the author combines intimate story-telling with profound questions about living up to the Great American ideals. This book is reminiscent of the stories of other champions with whom I have had the honor of working."

CAPRICE TAYLOR MENDEZ, LA VOZ HISPANA RADIO HOST, ADJUNCT PROFESSOR OF PEACE AND CONFLICT STUDIES AT GATEWAY COMMUNITY COLLEGE

"Sherman understands the power of prevention over intervention, of human connection, of asking the right questions, and of always centering people's well-being in decision-making. *Chasing Social Justice* beautifully delivers pragmatic advice from her own experiences that makes disentangling the web of inequity seem possible, and absolutely worthwhile."

YASMINA VINCI, EARLY CHILDHOOD EXPERT AND CHILD/FAMILY ADVOCATE

"Honest, critical, and inspirational, *Chasing Social Justice* shows that we still live in a community of the people, by the people, and for the people. I hope professors use this with undergraduate and graduate students in a range of fields – from organizational development to public health, from education to political science."

PAUL J. HUTCHINSON, SENIOR LECTURER, BOSTON UNIVERSITY QUESTROM SCHOOL OF BUSINESS

Chasing
SOCIAL JUSTICE

How Do We Advance the Work that Matters Most?

BY LAURIE SHERMAN

MASLAN
HOUSE

Produced and Published by MASLAN HOUSE

www.ChasingSocialJustice.com

Paperback ISBN 978-0-578-67677-7
eBook ISBN 978-0-578-69052-0
Printed in the United States

For Dad, the late Lee Sherman, who almost never agreed with me politically, but insisted affectionately decades ago, "You've got a lot to say, kiddo; promise me you'll write a book some day."

For Mom, Marge Levy, whose values I strive to live by and pass on.

For two dear men, Arthur Levine and Jim Doscher. Arthur, my lifelong friend, your words of wisdom bolstered me. You reminded me not to try to write a book someone would want to publish, but to write what I wanted to say, and write the book I would want to read. My Jim, I thank you for so much. Your tough love kept me on track to finish.

CONTENTS

*Tell me, what is it you plan to do with your
one wild and precious life?*

−MARY OLIVER

direct

Introduction
WHERE CAN WE MAKE A DIFFERENCE?

The first time I remember thinking about social justice, I was eight years old, a recent arrival to a Wisconsin town called Brookfield. Before that, my family lived right outside New York City. Most people in my childhood neighborhoods were Jewish, proudly and comfortably so. I stood out a bit, though, with my white-blonde hair and blue eyes. Non-Jews never guessed I was Jewish, and even fellow Jews needed convincing: *Which of your parents is Jewish? Really? Both of them?*

In 1970, Mom, Dad, my brothers, and I piled into our aging brown station wagon for the two-day drive to the Midwest. The change was supposedly driven by Dad's job, but I think Mom was also relieved to put some miles between us and her loving but hovering Orthodox parents, who were living in Queens and running a small pharmacy.

While I relished the adventure of a long-distance move, and became fast friends with the girl next door, one part of my new life came as a shock: almost no one in this place was Jewish. Okay, make that *no one*. My brother Jeff was the only other Jew in my elementary school.

"Menorah, what's a menorah?" I remember one boy saying after my upbeat classroom show-and-tell of the silver candelabra. "Sounds like manure," he sneered. Many of my classmates, it turned out, had never heard of Chanukah. Shocked, defensive, I wanted to blurt out, *Do you really believe a fat man in a red suit flies around the world delivering presents down your chimney?* Thankfully my big brothers had taught me to hold my tongue.

It was unnerving, my schoolmates' comments and my new awareness of difference.

I went to one of the places where I'd always felt comfortable no matter where we lived — the library. I asked the lean, kind, dark-haired lady to recommend a book with a Jewish character. She handed me *The Diary of Anne Frank*.

As I opened Anne's journal each night, feelings coursed through me, confused about the dissonance between what I was reading and what I had always been taught: all people are equal. I would lie in bed, tired, in that state somewhere between asleep-dreaming and awake-imagining, wondering if Nazis would come to my country. In my mind, I could hear it: a break-in. Soldiers storm my house. I rush under the bed. They search the room for me. I watch their boots go by, heart pounding. But they find me; three big men in stiff uniforms drag me out.

But I tell myself, *Keep breathing. I am okay. I can pretend not to be Jewish; no one ever thinks I am. I have the cloak of my coloring. They might even believe me to be a nice Aryan girl. Right? Right?*

I can remember what it felt like, climbing back into bed after acting out this scene. Pulling up the covers, safe for that moment, I wondered aloud a question that haunts people around the world today: Is it okay to lie about who I am in order to save myself? What about saving other people?

I was asking, in my childlike way, How do I use the power that I have? And why isn't the world fair and safe?

Throughout my life I have felt a yearning to understand and advance social justice. What *is* social justice? I don't think of it as a noun, but a process and a perspective: seeing the potential and humanity in every person, starting from the understanding that no one is the same and each of us is inherently equal. Pursuing social justice is to remove barriers to people being safe and having the freedom that allows them to reach their potential. *Justice* can be something we pursue for an individual (someone who has been wronged, or, conversely, someone who has wrongfully been convicted of a wrong-doing); whereas *social justice* we pursue for entire segments of our population. It is the pursuit of justice for the sake of a society.

For me, pursuing social justice is also not an isolated endeavor. The lessons I have learned from working in movements and organizations have informed the other aspects of my life — parenting, intimate relationships, friendships, and my efforts to be a good neighbor, a good daughter to my parents, and a good sister to my brothers.

I DON'T THINK OF SOCIAL JUSTICE AS A NOUN, BUT A PROCESS AND A PERSPECTIVE: SEEING THE POTENTIAL AND HUMANITY IN EVERY PERSON, STARTING FROM THE UNDERSTANDING THAT NO ONE IS THE SAME AND EACH OF US IS INHERENTLY EQUAL.

I often wonder, for all of us involved in health and social services, or active in different movements, when does our sense of justice versus injustice emerge? Is it a slow awakening or a sudden jolt? Does it result from something that happens to us or what we see happening to others? For me it was a combination.

Four years after the Wisconsin move, followed by a stint in Illinois, we relocated again, finishing the drive across the country, landing in the San Francisco suburb of San Mateo. Again I was the new kid in town. I started to grasp the complexities of standing up for others and standing up for myself. Now age 12, I faced a mix of what today we could call bullying and hazing. One component of the hazing: three kids would sit behind me on the school bus, holding a packet of matches close to the ends of my long hair, threatening to light me on fire. Instinctively, I knew my job was to sit still, not blink, squirm, or react in any way. I pulled it off, at first. My heart was almost bursting out of my chest from fear, but I refused to show it. Only able to bear this for a few weeks and too humiliated to tell my family, I borrowed a bike and began getting myself to school.

I still got picked on here and there. I was an average-sized kid, so potentially big enough to fight back, but I faced the dilemma of not knowing if that would make things better or worse. One day, one of the tougher girls from school saw I had a flat tire on my bike. She followed me for a few blocks. Once we were out of sight of both the adults and other kids, she kicked me over and over from behind as I pushed the bike, saying crazy, made-up stories about things I had done to deserve it. As with the lighter on the bus, I was determined not to let her win by seeing me react. For many years after, the memories still with me, I would wish I had turned around and slugged her. Heck, I occasionally used to dream about beating the shit out of her. But at the time, I feared she would just retaliate by bringing more kids to get me. One problem with not fighting back, for any of us who have faced bullying, is it's easy to turn the bad thoughts against ourselves if we don't turn them outwards by pushing back. On some level I wondered what was wrong with me. Over time, though, as I developed deeper curiosity and empathy, the bad dreams stopped; I began to wonder who had been kicking her to the point where she felt she needed to kick someone else.

Eventually, most of the bullying stopped, perhaps because I wasn't reacting, perhaps because I had developed some cred as a result of my stoicism. As a white kid from a relatively middle-class family (we had the basics we needed, but spent a brief time on food stamps when my father lost his job), I quickly noticed the other newcomers and outsiders at my middle school. In addition to wanting to protect myself from bullying, I wanted to protect them. Something inside me early on said that it's our responsibility to see each other, to care for each other, to stand up for each other.

Tiny, curly-haired Zaida was taunted at recess for being from another country. She was so beautiful and kind, I thought, how could they do that to her? I knew I had few fighting skills, but I stepped in front of her one day, to protect Zaida, figuring I'd at least earn her friendship, which I did. She took me to visit her apartment, filled with love from many siblings and Mexican relatives, as well as the inviting smells of foods I had not tasted before.

Then Carrie, whose family was Filipino, turned to us for friendship when she realized someone might listen non-judgmentally. She felt powerless; her mom was long gone, and when her dad drank, he beat up her older sister. It was my first exposure to someone feeling not just unsafe at *school*, as I did, but unsafe at *home*. That seemed so wrong to me.

I also got to know Keiko, who always went by Katherine at school, working hard to hide that her parents didn't speak English. I could tell she was afraid of seeming even more different than she was already perceived to be. And my other new friend, Mary. Pale-skinned, freckle-faced, with a dazzling grin, Mary was large, strong, and a competitive athlete, so I couldn't imagine she would be afraid of anything. But her whole demeanor changed every time we walked into their apartment. When she saw her stepfather, the fear was palpable.

Despite our disparate backgrounds, all of us were drawn to each other by our love of learning, each a proud nerd with a goofy spirit and a desire to question life's rules. As I realized these kids weren't just different from me and different from each other, but that they were living with fears I hadn't experienced, my sense of justice and injustice grew more sophisticated. While I experienced fear during the two years in San Mateo from the bullying, I also realized how fortunate I was to have a safe home and loving parents, who eventually divorced but each stayed in my life.

Flash forward. I headed from California to Rhode Island, fortunate to land a spot at Brown University and even more fortunate to land a huge financial aid package and some private scholarships from essay contests, without which I could not have attended. When I first arrived at the storied campus in Providence — oh my. I had no idea about concepts like the wealth gap. Mom and I didn't think it made sense for her to spend the money on an extra ticket, so I flew on my own to New York, then took the train up to Providence. Most of the other students arrived with their families and much more than my one small trunk.

I walked into the dorm to meet my roommate Debbie and her parents and thought, *It's a good thing I like the color blue!* They had arrived two days before, painted the room pale blue, put in wall-to-wall bright blue shag carpet, purchased a fridge (which no one had in those days), put up royal blue curtains, and installed a folding door down the middle of the room, so that when she got dressed, my roommate could close it for privacy! Although we were from different worlds, Debbie was smart and funny, and we enjoyed each other's company. I shook my head in amusement as she called her mom every day, which was crazy expensive back then. I was raised so independently that it wouldn't even have occurred to me to want to talk to Mom more than once a month.

As the fall went on, I started to get used to the family income disparities I saw around me — after some initial shocks, that is. Some kids actually brought new cars to school! I literally knew no friends from home whose parents had ever bought them a car.

I had been offered a job by the school as part of my aid package, and was looking forward to it. Work had always grounded me, from a stint delivering newspapers in middle school to cleaning the house of the elderly man next door to us in high school, thrilled to feel the $20 bill in my hand every Sunday.

I didn't know until I got to Brown that most of the students wouldn't be working. While it wasn't a luxurious role, loading the huge industrial dishwasher in the basement of the main dining hall, I actually liked the job. The other students and supervisors were friendly, and the 15 hours per week gave me structure. Sometimes the job included collecting dishes left in the dining hall upstairs. One day, I was cleaning off a table where a bunch of expensively dressed kids were sitting, and I bumped into JFK Jr. I had heard he was coming to Brown my same year. It's funny, the things that stick with us. I remember he was kind and respectful to me as I cleared the dishes, making eye contact and saying hello, talking normally, whereas most of his tablemates took no notice of "the help."

So although I was getting used to these differences among the students, I thought my hearing must be wrong when, as Thanksgiving approached, Debbie said her father was turning 50 and flying 50 friends to an island to celebrate, on a private plane. Here I was trying to figure out where to spend Thanksgiving, since it was too expensive to go home to California.

Once I did get home for the longer winter break and told my mom how weird that all was, her voice grew firm and serious. *Uh oh, a life lesson is coming.* Mom said she didn't want to hear me even start down some ridiculous path of feeling sorry for myself. Compared to most of the country, and certainly most of the world, she said, we are well off. We have everything we need. How could I go to school at a place like Brown and even entertain the idea that I didn't have enough? She was having none of it! It was one of those times it really hit me really hard that people tend to look up — at what others have — and not look around to what others don't. (Another time was as an adult. An old friend from high school said, "It's not like I am rich or something," when I let my jaw drop after seeing his huge house with an even huger yard and built-in pool, and heard about his twice-annual family trips on vacations abroad, as well as putting their kids in private school. I can't remember if I said it out loud or simply thought it: *If you're not rich, buddy, then who is?*)

After my mom's admonishment, my embarrassment for thinking I deserved sympathy faded pretty quickly, and I felt gratitude for my family, our apartment, clothes, food, friends, books, and school. Then I thought, *How do we make sure everyone has these?*

The draw to social justice work is different for each person. We ought to ponder what drives us, so we can be effective but also check ourselves — our perspective, our motives. I've realized my passion comes from a mix of facts and feelings. The facts: How can it not eat at us that the United States is nowhere near as fair as it purports to be, given how many people are suffering in this land of plenty? The feelings: As strong a person as I am, I embody an echo of fragility — from the moving, the bullying, the times my family was financially insecure — that drives me to want to help others.

The students I was drawn to at Brown shared my concern for justice, although they gently teased me about the melodramatic ways I expressed my growing political awareness, with letters to the school newspaper that began, "I am appalled!" I wrote one when ardently anti-feminist Phyllis Schlafly was invited to speak on campus and was to be paid significantly more than her debate opponent. My friends Kate, Arthur, Cindy, and Jane taught me about issues I had never been exposed to, such as access to birth control and safe abortion.

We were an ambitious, idealistic quintet. Among the four of them was a literature major on a path to becoming a university professor; two budding scientists planning to attend med school and rock the world of ob-gyn research and pediatric health policy; and a writer who aimed to be an editor and diversify the characters in children's books. Our undergrad output included a how-to-manual on women's rights, a book of poetry (with pieces about same-sex relationships, a hush-hush topic back then); prizes in biology and religion; and recognition for community service, including at a shelter for domestic violence survivors.

Cindy's mom Nancy sat with the five of us not long before our college graduation. A social worker and general rabble-rouser throughout her life, Nancy's eyes twinkled, listening to us wax poetic about our passions, our hopes for the future, our grandiose plans to change the world.

Puffing her way through a pack of cigarettes, Nancy posited that one of our tasks in life would be to figure out not only what issues to take on, but in what arena to operate — neighborhood? national? international? She encouraged us to take time to explore what realm would be large enough for us to have an impact, and yet small enough to see, to really *know*, we were making a difference. Think about where you can contribute, she said, and where you will find meaning. And for God's sake, she added, don't take yourselves so seriously. With that, she put out her cigarette and grinned her way through a favorite quote:

> *Dear Pessimist, Optimist, and Realist,*
> *While you were busy arguing over whether the glass is half*
> *empty or half full, I drank it.*
> *Signed,*
> *The Opportunist*

I chose the citywide arena. Following college, I spent 12 years in the nonprofit world and then took a role advising Mayor Thomas Menino, early on in what would become his 20-year tenure as Boston's longest-serving mayor. I focused on child and family policy, developing educational initiatives aimed at breaking cycles of poverty. After seeing me moderate a complex political forum, Mayor Menino plucked me from a position running a public health coalition in a neighborhood of Boston that was home to immigrants speaking more than 21 languages; he said he wanted more people in his administration coming from outside government, with different ideas and experiences.

Prior to that health coalition where I met Tom Menino, I worked in the movement to prevent the spread of HIV, after running a community newspaper. Along the way, I devoted time in either paid or volunteer work to domestic violence, lesbian and gay issues, and education for children with disabilities. Today, I serve as executive vice president of Thompson Island Outward Bound Education Center, a nonprofit that strives to close the achievement gap with middle schoolers through outdoor science infused with Outward Bound's approach to developing leadership and commitment to service.

These 35 years in the nonprofit field, community organizing, and government work have afforded me an opportunity to spend time with leaders at many levels in and around Boston, as well as in other large and small cities. I've faced challenges across multiple fields of service and have gained an understanding of what can (and what doesn't) work to alter seemingly hopeless situations.

Chasing Social Justice is a collection of my lessons learned, primarily focused on the three and a half decades from the Reagan administration to the exit of Barack Obama and the emergence of Donald Trump. I am not writing about child welfare or health care access or affordable housing or marriage equality or gun control or education reform. I write about child welfare *and* health care access *and* affordable housing *and* marriage equality *and* gun control *and* education reform. What can we learn across movements, campaigns, organizations? Where is our work hitting the mark, and where are we falling short? How do we make a sustainable difference, and how do we keep on keeping on?

Boston, where much of my work has taken place, is a fascinating case study, given its size (big but not huge); its extraordinary diversity of residents (across race, culture, religion, socio-economic status, ethnicity, and language); and its embrace both of history and of recent innovation (with a concentration of universities, hospitals, and tech companies). Boston's challenges are representative of major issues facing cities around the nation.

As the site of the American Revolution, home to the first public library, and the birthplace of public education, Boston has been a good place for me to reflect on social justice and on the many complexities obscured by the country's recent polarization. Our constitution was written based on awe-inspiring ideals, and yet long before that, the country was "discovered" by those who poisoned and slaughtered the indigenous peoples. What do we make of that contrast? The United States has incredible potential, yet at the same time, our not-so-united nation is nowhere near as fair and safe, peace-promoting, or forward-thinking as it could — and must — be.

These are the kinds of questions that have gnawed at me throughout my career: Why don't we enact more practical policies that reflect our stated values, especially when they would cost *less*, not more? Why are we still talking about many crucial social and political issues in the same ways we did decades ago? Why do we take a key step forward as they do in other countries — in childcare quality or gun control, for example — and then, unlike other countries, we get stuck, or even end up one or two steps back? One saying at my kids' elementary school was that smart is not what you *are*; it's what you choose to *become*. Since every child can choose to get smarter every day, can't we grownups? Can't our country?

The most important lesson I've learned across workplaces and movements, as we take on complex and intractable problems, is that we must start by asking the right questions and resist the powerful urge to simplify and polarize. We often ask the wrong questions, those that lead to a dead end. When we ask the right ones, we are able to move toward approaches that illuminate real and sustainable solutions to improve opportunity and ensure equity. Throughout *Chasing Social Justice*, I offer concepts, specific strategies, and questions that have been effective in strengthening organizations and movements. I do this mainly through storytelling; in the end, given the nuances of the social issues we face, no matter our degrees, none of us is an expert as much as we are a storyteller. I think of activists as artists with a palette, painting a dream in a way that makes it visible for others, in turn opening doors and hearts.

> THE MOST IMPORTANT LESSON I'VE LEARNED ACROSS WORKPLACES AND MOVEMENTS IS THAT WE MUST START BY ASKING THE RIGHT QUESTIONS, WHICH HELPS US TO RESIST THE POWERFUL URGE TO SIMPLIFY AND POLARIZE.

I don't underestimate how hard it is to promote effective and complex dialogue, and for that dialogue actually to produce a change in policy and behavior. This is hard work, often without obvious progress until suddenly, a light flickers. I never fail to be surprised and moved by what happens when we follow the best of the advice I offer here — and I never fail to feel frustration when I forget to heed what I've learned! I think back to the efforts I have been part of, sometimes successful, sometimes failed, to build bridges — between Black and Jewish leaders, between a group of African American women and white women who viewed feminism differently, between immigrants from many countries and the long-time Irish residents who were offended that "those people" had arrived in "their" neighborhood.

I reflect also on conversations between Christian clergy who opposed marriage equality and Jewish same-sex couples who met with them to share their personal stories, and between advocates for teen programming and advocates for younger children who realized it was ridiculous to compete for a too-small piece of the pie. I have experienced the impact of facilitating successful workshops to encourage middle-class parents not to rule out public education without first investigating the local schools. I have had the privilege of participating in state Department of Children and Families case reviews to discern whether children in foster care could safely be returned home, and I saw how advocates used the lessons from those sessions to change human service policies for kids aging out of the foster care system. I learned from running trainings to help mothers with AIDS decide how to tell their stories in order to combat misunderstandings about the epidemic, while maintaining privacy and integrity as they prepared to die.

These past three decades have felt like a train ride through varied social justice terrain, with views that range from bleak to stunning. Rosie from Mexico coming up to me after a coalition meeting to say she felt welcome in her neighborhood for the first time, even though she had immigrated 10 years before. A handsome Black man and his dashing Italian boyfriend strolling gleefully out of Boston City Hall, holding up their marriage license on the first day that same-sex couples could apply in Massachusetts. A woman sprawled out in pain on the floor of a supermarket after a seizure, speaking into her cell phone to convince her boss from one of her two jobs that she truly could not come in to work. A colleague suddenly leaning forward to ask a candidate we were interviewing for a major education initiative, "Why do you think people are poor?"

Cuddling up to read a book one night, years back, my youngest murmured, "I love you Mommy. I love you so much I want to marry you when I grow up . . . But you'll be dead."

Even when my kids don't casually call out my mortality, I think about what we are passing on to the next generation, what lessons learned, and how we might hasten the pace of our change efforts.

One answer is to fight those natural tendencies to oversimplify and polarize. Affirmative action — it's the solution ... or the problem itself. Abortion — murder or basic right. Capital punishment — essential deterrent or unacceptable cruelty. Elder care — the responsibility of all or an utterly private concern. In public education, standardized testing is either a brilliant stroke of accountability or the death of innovation; charter schools are either sink holes that bankrupt traditional public education or the only chance to save "failing schools." Marriage equality — it's a civil right ... or the end of civilization!

I am not arguing that the answer is for all of us to compromise our values and settle on some sort of amorphous middle ground. I am a strong believer in marriage equality as well as the inherent right for women to control their bodies and their health care. In fact, too often it is marginalized or oppressed people who have been asked to wait patiently or to consider other viewpoints, as when President Trump indicated that white supremacist views are as valid as the views of those trying to stem violence against people of color. There must be no middle ground on many things. As James Baldwin said, "We can disagree and still love each other, unless your disagreement is rooted in my oppression and denial of my humanity and right to exist."

> THERE MUST BE NO MIDDLE GROUND ON MANY THINGS. AS JAMES BALDWIN SAID: "WE CAN DISAGREE AND STILL LOVE EACH OTHER, UNLESS YOUR DISAGREEMENT IS ROOTED IN MY OPPRESSION AND DENIAL OF MY HUMANITY AND RIGHT TO EXIST."

I do believe, though, that when we start to listen more than we talk, when we make a true effort to understand the fears that come up for those who disagree with us, when we look for true common ground on which to build, and when we deploy lessons learned from successful movements, we have an incredible shot at achieving justice.

The lessons I've learned about how to pursue social justice are not, as they say, rocket science. Some, you will see, are even common sense.

Sometimes we find that change is achingly slow; other times it surprises us with its speed. Sometimes the change comes about when we combine somber work with levity, as in a bumper sticker I spotted during the marriage equality debates: "If you want gay people to stop having sex, let them get married."

My hope is that *Chasing Social Justice* will aid in your own quest to leave our country better than you found it, and to take care of yourself along the way, so that you have the energy to remain a change-maker and truth-teller throughout your life, in the arena that makes sense for you. Let's continue the chase together.

Chapter 1
WHAT'S IN A NAME?

Not everything that is faced can be changed,
but nothing can be changed if it isn't faced.
-JAMES BALDWIN

One day in February of 2009, I morphed into a cartoon character. Sometimes the absurdities in our culture knock me off my feet, and to get back up I don a figurative cape embroidered with *ML* — mortified liberal.

This time it was at a public school in Hayward, California, outside San Francisco. My older brother Jeff, an award-winning middle school teacher, invited me to help him honor the seventh and eighth graders who had earned As and Bs throughout the year at Martin Luther King Middle School, where he taught. He thought they might like to hear from an advisor to an East Coast mayor, plus he wanted me to help break up the reading of the 100 honorees by alternating my voice with his.

Such joy and energy and pride filled the room. I noticed that first. The next thing I noticed was that the faces in the auditorium were almost entirely black or brown, with some Asian students and a few white kids. And the third thing I noticed: The list Jeff gave me to read featured names I had never heard of, not to mention pronounced before — first names like Xochil and Jaskeerat; last names such as Soukhaseun, Jaochico, Ocequeda, and Kaleohano. He handed me the list at the microphone right as the event began. Thanks bro!

After doing my best with pronunciation (not wanting to bungle this important moment for the honorees), feeling jazzed by shaking the hands of these proud students who came on stage to accept their awards, I got to address the audience. I asked what they would say if they could talk directly to President Obama's then-Education Secretary, Arne Duncan, who used to run the public school system in Chicago. Arms flew in the air. Smart, assertive, funny kids. "The arts matter and all our programs have been cut." "I'd tell him our teachers are great but we need more of them." "We can't afford sports uniforms." "We want more advanced classes." "Please tell him that kids these days *do* care."

After the assembly, Jeff walked me back to the classroom to speak more intimately with students in his US History class, all eighth graders, 13 and 14 years old. I was taken aback by the packed classroom and did a quick head count: 35 kids. "Jeff, do you have an aide or an intern or co-teacher?" I asked. Nope. One teacher, 35 students.

The ML cape materialized. It's not that I didn't know many places in the country have ridiculous teacher-student ratios; I just hadn't seen it up close in a while. Long before I flew across the country to visit him, Jeff had told me stories about his students, kids who come from homes that range from poor to middle-income, many with only one parent because the father had either left or died. Many of his students were being raised by parents who never finished high school and so were less equipped to help their children with homework. Many had older siblings who had already given up on beating the odds, already dropped out, or were pregnant. Some of the students had come from other countries and only learned English in the past few years.

These are the kids, I stood there thinking, who have to compete with 34 peers for their teacher's attention? Ten or twenty miles away in an economically well-off suburb, public school students who struggle with none of those particular barriers might have 10 fewer in their classroom. And other kids might have it even better, at a private school, like the ones near me in Boston, 2 or 3 adults in a classroom with 16 or 18 kids — as low as a 1 to 8 ratio, versus this 1 to 35. Where the hell, I thought, are our priorities as a country? What kind of rabbits are we expecting urban public school teachers to pull out of their hats?

I asked Jeff's students what they thought of class size inequity. They jumped out of their seats with opinions. They asked what my mayor had done about class size. Boston has reduced it, I told them. Boston class sizes for the lower grades went from 28 kids to 22 over a seven-year period in the late 90s (a 20 percent reduction) and class size under Mayor Menino was not raised back even in tough economic times. I told Jeff's students that in Brookline, an ethnically mixed but well-off town next to Boston, the leaders got brave and did something logical: they made the honors classes *larger* and *reduced* the class size in the courses for kids who are struggling. Think about it, I said to them, students who are excelling and have chosen to be in an advanced class don't need quite the one-on-one that a child who is struggling needs. But in many school systems the "gifted" and advanced classes are the smallest. Go figure.

During the conversation, I couldn't help but look at these young teens and see their promise, but also what they would be off to encounter next in the world, the barriers we are expecting them to leap. It was one of those moments where all the professional work I do doesn't matter, and the intellectual arguments seem irrelevant; I felt sick to my stomach about our country's priorities. It's how public school teachers tell me they feel much of the time.

At the end, I asked the students to sit quietly for one minute and just think to themselves: *What is one thing I am going to do in my life to help this country become more fair?* It wasn't so different from the charge the school's assistant principal gave the group of 100 at Jeff's honors assembly earlier in the day: "Together you represent one-fifth of this school. Next year I want to have twice the number of students here. There is no reason half the school, or even the whole school, can't achieve all As and Bs. I want each of you to pick two friends who have the potential to earn higher grades but need some motivation, and I want *you* to help them make sure they get here next year." It was a great speech by their school leader, but even as I myself challenged the students to think about their role and responsibility, I knew that we can't put it all on the kids.

We don't have to know all the answers before we name the problems we are facing as a country. The challenge is that, conversely, if we don't even name our problems, we'll never make progress. Physicians need a diagnosis to determine the treatment regimen; therapists will similarly explain that sometimes simply correctly naming a problem — seeing it clearly — creates space for solutions one couldn't have imagined otherwise.

When I met those kids in California, it became clear to me that the commitment to educational equity varies significantly from state to state, even county to county; we do not have a unified policy as a country. To accelerate the progress of improving public education for everyone, which is the primary way out of poverty for those born into it, we must name the dramatic difference in the education kids are receiving in the US, based almost solely on their zip code.

> WE DON'T HAVE TO KNOW ALL THE ANSWERS BEFORE WE NAME THE PROBLEMS WE ARE FACING AS A COUNTRY. THE CHALLENGE IS THAT, CONVERSELY, IF WE DON'T EVEN NAME OUR PROBLEMS, WE'LL NEVER MAKE PROGRESS.

In Boston, as the birthplace of public education, one would think these conversations would be robust, and sometimes they are, whether led by a businessperson, a political leader or a representative of a forward-thinking foundation. To his credit, Mayor Menino declared in his third State of the City address in 1996 that he wanted to be judged by the progress, or lack thereof, of the school system during his tenure. In his memoir *Mayor for a New America*, published upon his retirement, Mayor Menino cited a declaration from the Boston town meeting of 1784, the ambitious original vision for public education:

> *That the common school should serve the Benefit of the Poor and the Rich; that the Children of all, partaking of equal Advantages and being placed upon an equal Footing, no Distinction might be made among them in the Schools on account of the different Circumstances of their Parents, but that the Capacity and natural genius of each might be cultivated and improved for the future benefit of the whole Community.*

Class size is one of the biggest differences in schools that serve kids growing up in poverty versus schools serving kids growing up with great economic resources. One common response to the effort to reduce class size in poorer communities is that it doesn't make enough of a difference in academic outcomes unless you get the teacher-student ratio all the way down from 1:30 to 1:15. So let's go all the way down to 1:15.

The next retort is that we can't afford it. It is a worthy and complex conversation to debate the best uses of our tax dollars and the best return on investment for different education interventions, captured well in an analysis by the non-partisan think tank the Brookings Institute entitled "Class Size: What Research Says and What it Means for State Policy."[1] And yet it is painful to note that well-off communities don't agonize over the complexities of the research; they simply ensure their kids have a small class size. And let's remember that this country has always found money for certain priorities, such as the still deeply troubling war in Iraq from 2003 to 2011. The US involvement there took the lives of 4,500 US soldiers (impacting tens of thousands of their family members, including leaving thousands of children without one or both parents), as well as injuring another 30,000 Americans. The death toll of Iraqi civilians was estimated to range from 184,000 to 207,000. The financial cost thus far: $2.4 *trillion* and growing, if we (as we should) provide lifetime services to all veterans who returned injured from that war. Had we foregone that war, those funds could have permanently reduced every public school classroom in the entire United States to a maximum of 15 students, via short-term outlays to school systems and an education investment strategy with a percentage of the funds.

In a country that insists everyone is equal and can rise above any rough beginnings simply based on their own hard work, honestly, how can we tolerate such obvious inequities facing children when they enter kindergarten? We have the capacity to address the problem by following plain mathematical funding formulas. But before we can even hope to get to solutions, we've got to agree there *is* a problem.

For years in the US, talk about poverty subsided, as if it no longer mattered as a national conversation or as if it were a politically incorrect topic. Thankfully, discussions about economic inequality rose again, especially during the 2016 presidential primary, and have continued in recent years. Yet we're just beginning to acknowledge how little economic mobility currently exists in the US, as compared to our past.

This table published in the *Washington Post* in October of 2014[2] illustrates a mind-boggling reality: in this land of opportunity, a child born into poverty who obtains a *college degree* has the same likelihood of earning low wages as a *high school dropout* who was born well-off, as shown by the horizontal arrow. Conversely, the vertical arrow illustrates that a high school dropout who was born into wealth is as likely to be among the top wage earners of his peers as a person born into poverty who completes her college education.

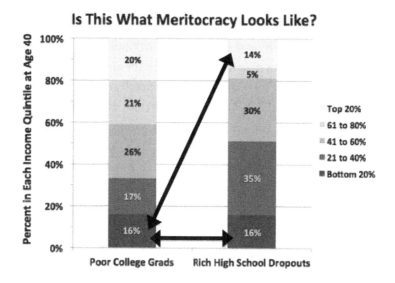

Author Matt O'Brien titled his article that featured the table "Poor Kids Who Do Everything Right Don't Do Better Than Rich Kids Who Do Everything Wrong." O'Brien explains that it is as much about glass floors and glass walls as glass ceilings:

"Rich kids who can go work for the family business or inherit the family estate don't need a high school diploma to get ahead. It's an extreme example of what economists call "opportunity hoarding." That includes everything from legacy college admissions to unpaid internships that let affluent parents rig the game a little more in their children's favor. But even if they didn't, low-income kids would still have a hard time getting ahead. That's, in part, because they're targets for diploma mills that load them up with debt, but not a lot of prospects."

Facing this kind of research, we can then go deeper, understanding that institutionalized racism must be named. How is it possible that some school systems are more segregated now than when *Brown v. Board of Education* was decided? What is the history and long-term impact of redlining? How have funding formulas, such as the reliance on property taxes to fund education, supported white-dominant schools over others? We have to look at the research showing that children of color are more quickly labeled as emotionally disturbed or suspended for the same behavior as a white peer.

In his 2014 book *The Opportunity Equation: How Citizen Teachers Are Combating the Achievement Gap in America's Schools*, Eric Schwarz names a problem. He says our continued focus on what happens inside classrooms misses a significant factor in educational equity: what happens in kids' lives *outside* the classroom. In 1995, Schwarz co-founded Citizen Schools, a nonprofit originally based in Boston that helps teenagers across the country through extended day programs. Schwarz's book highlights examples of successful ways to address this "opportunity gap." The gap refers to the fact that by age 12, kids from low-income and poor families have had 6,000 fewer hours of out-of-school education opportunities as compared to kids from middle- and upper-income families.[3] In those thousands of hours, kids born into privilege get a huge leg up in their education through summer camps, paid tutors, sports programs, visits to museums, travel, science fairs, arts programs.[4]

When I met with Schwarz, he agreed that naming this gap (what happens to kids in grades K–12 when they are not in the classroom) and its relationship to economic immobility is a key to addressing the associated problems, such as those illustrated in the table. I shared my perspective that we also need to look at two other gaps that must be named and addressed: what happens to kids before they enter a classroom in the first place (*the pre-school gap*) and what relationship our students' families do or do not have with the schools while kids are there (*the parent-school connection gap*). I believe that the only way we will see improved and *sustainable* educational outcomes is to focus simultaneously on the school system *and* all three of these gaps.

When we are talking about education, naming a problem is different from pointing fingers, standing back to assign blame, as in the term "failing schools." Certainly, some schools are weak — that includes district public schools, charter schools, private schools, parochial schools, urban schools, suburban schools, rural schools. But the blanket attacks on public school teachers and the simplistic idea that what goes on inside schools has nothing to do with external factors leaves us stuck — and polarized.

One step to naming without blaming is to identify where we ourselves play a role in the problems and can make a difference in the solutions. After Mayor Menino stepped down in 2013, a field of 12 candidates vied to succeed him. Aching to keep a focus on public education, a culturally diverse group of six of us (who had been colleagues over the years) created the Boston Ed Blog, a short-term online forum to keep a focus on education throughout the mayoral race. In addition to soliciting reader questions for the candidates to answer about education, we each wrote pieces on aspects of education reform. But we agreed that we would only publish a blog post, by ourselves or a guest writer, that named a component of education that wasn't being talked about enough, that featured examples of what *is* working, and that included how we ourselves might be part of a solution.

For me, the most potent piece published on the Boston Ed Blog, which I then re-printed on my own blog[5], was by a low-income parent in our group. A native of Haiti, Mireille Louis identified the often simple, but highly effective steps taken by her daughter's school to help parents be engaged and involved. First Mireille acknowledged the internal struggles immigrant and/or low-income families like hers face:

> *Born in Haiti, the youngest of eleven kids, my parents moved us*
> *to the United States (New Jersey) when I was 11 and we settled*
> *in Boston when I was 22. My story is harder than some, easier*

than others. I count my blessings every day. And I struggle every day...

The way I see it, children are the seeds we plant. They are the flowers of our city, often surviving through storms that threaten to uproot them. Their struggles, and the struggles of their families, are the weeds we have to remove together.

I've always seen myself as my daughter's "teacher" and educational partner; it's just how we think in Haiti. From the time my daughter was conceived, I read to her. As a single mom, even when I was tired from a long day of working a ten- or twelve-hour shift as a full-time assistant store manager, I read to her every morning and every evening. In the daytime, she stayed home with my elderly parents, who spoke to her in the only language they knew: Haitian Creole.

Once my daughter turned 3, I wanted her to be in a place where she could interact with other kids. I applied to Head Start, but they said they had to turn me down. I had just been laid off and my unemployment check put me a few dollars over the requirement...

What do I see as the barriers for parents, when it comes to being involved in our children's education? For some immigrants (like me) and other minorities, it is hard, even if we understand and speak English, and especially if we don't. I would like for more of us to share our stories, so others can understand what grows and what is wilting from the heat in our gardens — to see if we have shared values, experiences and worries.

I guess the biggest barrier for me in supporting my daughter has been income level, not necessarily the fact of being an immigrant. Unemployed now, and without a car, and the only caretaker of my elderly mom and my young daughter, I just haven't been able to find work that allows me to get to the office AND to get to my family when they need me. Also, I still sometimes catch myself thinking that because we are not from a wealthy *family, maybe we don't have the right to dream big. I find it very hard to ask for help, since the minute you open that door, with those words, "I need…" you worry the person is already thinking less of you. But for my daughter to go to summer camp or take part in any sort of extracurricular activity, I always have to ask if there is a sliding scale or a scholarship. It's uncomfortable. But I want her to have the opportunities in order to keep up with her peers.*

Next Mireille named the steps her school takes that help reduce barriers:

1. *Parent engagement means making us feel welcome AT the school, from kindergarten all the way through high school.*
2. *It's also whether a school helps us understand how to support our children's learning at home.*
3. *Productive parent engagement is more likely to happen if we moms and dads and care providers have been involved in our kid's "education" at their preschool or childcare program, so we realize even before entering kindergarten that it's our role (and our right) to be a partner.*

What does this look like at my school?

- *My school's open door policy welcomes me to visit at any time (although I usually call ahead).*
- *Every summer the next teacher my daughter will have in September visits us in our home. Why can't that happen at more schools?*
- *Everyone in the school talks about all kids as scholars and owners of the school day. I can tell my child is respected there. Is this true for other schools?*
- *The school offers classes for parents on how to read to our children, on child behavior, family nutrition and financial literacy. When they do, they provide a meal and childcare and try to help us arrange car-pooling. I don't have a car and I wish transportation could be provided.*

- *They take parent-teacher conferences seriously. The teacher listens to my concerns, letting me take as long as I need with my questions. Then the teacher follows up with me 1-2 weeks later with a text message to see how things are going at home. I love that. It's free. Why don't more places do this?*

One reason we are hesitant to name some of the problems in education is the tendency to avoid frank conversation about race and class. It can be extremely uncomfortable to say it out loud. What's the *it* in this case? Educating poor children is difficult, because of the many extenuating circumstances surrounding their lives. Children growing up in poverty often come to school less prepared in their early years, often do not have the benefit of parents with leisure time to reinforce learning at home, or may be experiencing dire situations such as homelessness, lack of food, domestic violence, and crime in their neighborhood, all of which impact their ability to learn and often impact behavior as well. Children who are poor — of any race or culture — are more likely to be experiencing these challenges and are thus more challenging to educate.

So let's work harder at taking steps to improve their education while acknowledging their life challenges as we aim to reduce poverty in the first place. Socioeconomic integration is one approach urban school systems are trying, to improve educational outcomes for all students. In San Francisco, in order to achieve more socioeconomically integrated schools, the school choice system included a carrot along with any sticks; they poured additional resources into schools in lower-income neighborhoods. The changes — such as significantly increasing arts and enrichment courses and second-language instruction — drew middle-income parents to schools they might not have considered. The results are still being examined and critiqued. Some large cities, including Boston and New York, as well as some suburban systems, also offer school choice with specific features to draw a diverse group of students/families to each school. In the town of Montclair, New Jersey, every public school has a different focus, such as science or theatre. So when parents go to rank their public elementary and secondary school choices, families of different economic means may be drawn to the same school for its focus and forte.

Obviously, education is not the only arena in which a failure to name inequities prevents progress. The AIDS epidemic is an example of progress delayed by a reticence of those in power to name. When former President Reagan died, debate ensued about his legacy. Particularly painful for many people who worked to save lives during the earlier years of the AIDS epidemic was the glossing over of his role in the public health crisis. They noted how, as the president when AIDS surfaced, he did not speak of the illness for many years, expressed ambivalence about whether kids with AIDS should be allowed to remain in school, and was slow to dedicate resources to the epidemic. What a contrast, I thought, when President Obama spoke openly and immediately about Ebola in 2014; he physically embraced a nurse returning to the US who had had Ebola, knowing that doing so on the world stage would help prevent stigma.

The early victims of AIDS were people often considered by mainstream society to be on the margins: gay and bisexual men, people who had injected drugs via hypodermic needles, and people of color — especially Haitians. It took years before many politicians were willing to stand up for AIDS prevention and treatment funding. I remember the painful references in the media to the "innocent" victims — hemophiliacs and children who got infected by infected mothers —which implied that other people with AIDS somehow deserved the disease.

I was in my 20s when the epidemic exploded. I was used to being an activist, on various social justice issues, so I was taken aback to find myself in a group being confronted by AIDS activists for not naming the problem.

It was 1987. The 10-person staff of *Gay Community News* (*GCN*), a weekly Boston-based newspaper dedicated to covering topics relevant to the national gay community, was holding its weekly meeting to review the latest edition. I was facilitating, as the Managing Editor. At 25 years old, I had found my way into the role after proving myself as the paper's advertising manager. I was in a bit over my head, but loving it and learning more by the day — business systems, fundraising for nonprofits, plus layout and design, back in the age of typesetting machines.

Founded in 1973, *GCN* was known as not only the first national gay newspaper, but also the most progressive, described as "the gay paper of record." The paid writers and volunteer contributors were a multi-racial crew and the paper was willing to cover anything and everything on the minds of gay activists and citizens. (Note: I use the term "gay" here because at that stage, LGBT was not a common phrase.)

In 1983, another weekly gay paper was launched in Boston, *Bay Windows*.

I WAS IN MY 20s WHEN THE AIDS EPIDEMIC EXPLODED. AS AN ACTIVIST ON VARIOUS SOCIAL JUSTICE ISSUES, I WAS TAKEN ABACK TO FIND MYSELF IN A GROUP BEING CONFRONTED BY AIDS ACTIVISTS FOR NOT NAMING THE PROBLEM.

It positioned itself as the paper for the "common gay person" (which many felt at the time was a euphemism for more upscale), those who didn't necessarily focus on being out, but simply living their lives. *GCN* was "We're here, we're queer, get used to it." *Bay Windows* was "We are your neighbors, your co-workers. We're just like you." Looking back, it was and is important to have these multiple perspectives, just as most cities have historically had more than one daily newspaper. But back then, with advertising dollars so tight and *GCN* always on the edge financially, it was quite threatening for *Bay Windows* to emerge.

So that day in the late 1980s, something happened that was unprecedented in the 14-year history of the paper. A group of gay men in their 20s and 30s walked into the office and disrupted our weekly staff meeting. They identified themselves as part of ACT UP, a national group formed to bring attention to the AIDS crisis emerging among gay and bisexual men. They wanted to know why *GCN* wasn't devoting more articles to AIDS, and they laid out their demands: they wanted us to devote one full-time writer to report on AIDS.

I was only 25, so I had a limited well of professional confidence and facilitation experience to draw from, but I did have decent judgment and basic skills. I knew it made more sense to listen than to try to force them to leave. I also knew we couldn't and shouldn't promise anything on the spot.

We let our own staff divisions surface, disagreeing in front of the protesters about the importance of AIDS and how women on staff felt about prioritizing the epidemic. Some of the staff team said resources are so tight we can't devote a full-time reporter to any one topic. One staffer noted that breast cancer affected lesbians at a higher rate than AIDS occurred in gay men, so why wouldn't we devote a reporter to that? We already do cover AIDS more than *Bay Windows*, one guy said — why aren't you confronting *them* instead of us, your own allies?

Their response to our arguments:

- Money (your newspaper budget) is never an excuse for not doing what is right.
- You are in denial about the severity of the epidemic.
- Exactly because you are our allies, we expect more of you than *Bay Windows*. You need to be the paper to name the epidemic and commit to covering it extensively until it ends.

They backed their demand with a threat: "If you do not create a plan to cover the AIDS epidemic widely and publicize this plan in the paper, we will begin a daily picket in front of the paper. You have one week." And they strode out.

While I disagreed with the threat component of their tactics, the ACT UP men did give me a wake-up call. I realized they were right: we hadn't been paying enough attention to this growing epidemic. *GCN*, of all publications, did indeed need to name the AIDS health problem in order to bring attention to it. We ran an editorial that week on AIDS and added a half-time reporter to focus solely on the epidemic.

At my next job, the epidemic again taught me something about naming.

Upon leaving *GCN* in 1988, I went into AIDS work myself. I was hired to expand a speakers bureau for the AIDS Action Committee, then the second largest AIDS organization in the world. This meant assembling a team of volunteers who would educate the public about preventing the spread of the disease and put a face on the diverse groups of people living with HIV, to help prevent discrimination. Every volunteer was required to go through a 40-hour training to understand the facts about the disease and improve their public speaking and teaching skills.

One of the people with AIDS who stepped up to be on the speakers bureau was a man named Sidney, for whom Sidney Borum Jr. Health Center was later named. When I met Sidney, long before he became a celebrity for his activism, he was a relatively shy, warm guy, a short, unassuming African American man living with HIV. As he went through my training and practiced how to tell his story, I noticed he did so in a self-derogatory way. We talked about it privately, and Sidney disclosed that he was bisexual, something not then typically accepted in the gay community or the Black community. His own discomfort about living outside the norm, without any sense of a community, made him not only hypersensitive to the reactions of others, but also self-critical and self-blaming. He believed it was his fault he got sick, even though he, like most people, knew nothing about HIV/AIDS when he contracted it, and he had never knowingly infected anyone else.

Our frank conversations about the sources of (and futility of) self-blame, combined with the training he received in public speaking, helped bring him out of his shell. Sidney eventually became a citywide leader, cited in the news for naming the impact of the epidemic on the Black community in particular, calling for more attention to racial and racist components of the epidemic. He also called out the Black community for not addressing their own discomfort with gay and bisexual members, noting that it led people to fail to seek treatment. Sidney named his own ambivalence and guilt about AIDS and then went on to name what had to change in the larger community.

Perhaps the best and best-known example of the impact of naming is the clergy sex abuse documented in the 2015 movie *Spotlight*. In 2001, the *Boston Globe*'s investigation team researched how many nearby Catholic priests had been accused, with substantiation, of sexual abuse of children. They uncovered 250 examples, many of which were covered up by the Archdiocese through moving the offender to a new church or making secret settlements. This travesty wasn't unique to Boston or to the US, and the reporting of it in that one location allowed for lawsuits and policy changes around the world, much of which is still in process.

Back to the question of class size I raised in the opening of this chapter, cape flowing across my back. As I told you, I visited my brother Jeff's classroom and saw he had 35 kids. Do you think it has gotten better, nationally? A spring 2018 article in the *Boston Globe*[6] named that the gap in spending across poorer versus richer communities on public education has actually grown wider. I paid close attention because the piece quoted a friend of mine who leads bike rides for a multicultural group in Boston. The article notes, "'The kids are the ultimate victims,' said Mark Richardson, a social studies and history teacher who delivers lessons to 41 students in a middle school library that has been converted into a classroom. 'It's a shame what is happening here.'"

What is the shame he references? Schools are still largely funded by property taxes. In a comparison of two districts just 30 miles apart, Brockton, where Mark teaches, has available to spend $14,778 per student, while Weston spends $24,458. Ironically, tragically, 70% of Brockton's students are economically disadvantaged, lack English fluency, or have disabilities, whereas in Weston only 24% of students face such challenges. So which kids need the resources more?

The article ends with even more disturbing numbers. Brockton spends $1.28 per student for supplies, while Weston spends $275.03. For technology, Brockton has $3.43 per student, while Weston has $210.56. In a country that says it stands for equal opportunity, there are no bootstraps, no boots, no socks for the kids in Brockton.

Even more absurd? On a bike ride a year after the article came out, Mark mentioned to me that his middle school class size occasionally hit 50. With one teacher.

To fend off being discouraged, I've seen activists use a combination of humor and sarcasm to name our shortfalls. One group protesting rape culture created a list of ten tips,[7] which went viral. The list was in response to the fact that young women are often given tips on how *they* can stop rape, rather than improving education and prevention with men. The list proposes pointers for people who might rape.

RAPE PREVENTION TIPS:

1. *Don't put drugs in a woman's drink.*
2. *Use the buddy system. If you are not able to stop yourself from assaulting people, ask a friend to stay with you while you are in public.*
3. *When you see a woman walking by herself, leave her alone.*
4. *Don't forget: it's not sex with someone who is asleep or unconscious; it's rape.*
5. *If you pull over to help a woman whose car has broken down, remember not to rape her.*
6. *Carry a whistle. If you are worried you might assault someone by accident, hand the whistle to the person so they can call for help.*
7. *If you are in an elevator and a woman gets in, don't rape her.*
8. *Honesty is the best policy. If you have the intention of having sex with someone you are going out on a date with regardless of her feelings about it, tell her there is every chance you will rape her. If you don't communicate your intentions, she may take it as a sign that you do not plan to rape her and inadvertently feel safe.*
9. *Never creep into a woman's home through the door or window, locked or unlocked, or spring out from behind parked cars, or rape her.*
10. *Don't rape.*

Steps like promoting this (intentionally absurd) list have been a part of the efforts that led to colleges instituting mandatory training on sexual harassment during orientation, and employers determining that staff must complete an online class to understand acceptable and unacceptable behaviors in the workplace, defining what sexual harassment looks like.

Naming oversized classes in Boston led to real solutions that made noticeable changes in the lives of residents. Similarly, giving AIDS attention as a growing and tragic national public health emergency led to research that led to medication and health education that changed behaviors, reducing the spread of the disease and providing a chance for people with HIV to survive.

Now we see people around the world naming the folly of ignoring or denying climate change, garnering media attention and building collaborations among scientists, young activists, and longtime global leaders. It is frightening to learn about the warming of our planet and powerful to see coalitions emerge to develop solutions. If we don't even name it, we surely can't fix it.

NOTES FOR THOSE PARTICULARLY
INTERESTED IN EDUCATION POLICY

The topic of naming came up for me when my boss, Mayor Tom Menino, stepped down in 2014. I decided to take time off to work on this book and to think beyond the realm of city education policy to the state level. Volunteering for Martha Coakley's gubernatorial campaign, I interviewed 19 people with various kinds of education expertise, including a fifth grade teacher at an inclusion school (where special education students learn alongside general education peers), the founder of a government department devoted to engaging immigrants and refugees in the life of the city, and Massachusetts state senator Tom Birmingham, one of the forces behind Massachusetts's original education reform bill, which dramatically increased funding for lower-income communities, along with accountability measures that would show how students from all cities and towns were learning. Here's what I learned was not being named, as I noted in my memos to the candidate:

1. *Students in private schools often experience a much richer and more holistic curriculum than students in public schools.* The approach public schools are taking to add back in more arts and other enrichment is too passive, because every time there is another budget crunch, those subjects (when considered stand-alone topics) will be cut. And the current tracking of "good" students into a college path and "weak" students into trades is a detriment to all, since tradespeople may choose to attend college and all students benefit from exposure to trades. We need a more robust approach to

ensure all students have a robust education. We could call that "an education that will LASTT" — meaning we need to infuse existing curriculum with Language learning, Arts, Sports, Trades, and Technology.

2. *In the debate over charter schools, it's important to acknowledge that the original intent was not for them to become widespread.* At least in Massachusetts, the education reform act of 1993 offered freedom from union rules and other restrictions in order to provide an opportunity to try new approaches that, if successful, would be shared with and replicated in more traditional public schools. The goal of the legislation was not to create a parallel system of separate public charter schools, in part because one of the working theories was that only through small-scale and non-bureaucratic experiments could ideas be cultivated that might impact the larger system. It may not be folly to expand charter schools with a new mandate, but current debate about them does not acknowledge that charter schools are veering dramatically from the original goal.

3. *The sharing of best practices is not happening between charter schools and traditional district public schools (also a goal of the original legislation), and it is not happening with other education systems.* I noted that no one was bringing together a wide range of educators and education systems to identify best practices to solve an agreed-upon set of challenges. The challenges to be discussed are how to expand the learning day and year in a cost-effective way; how to better engage parents and families in education; and how to create the

aforementioned kind of rich, integrated curriculum. It surprised me (and still does) that there are no statewide commissions that surface the proven approaches to these problems that are cost-effective, sustainable, and scalable, whether a solution is to be found in traditional or charter public schools, private schools, parochial schools, or even the home-schooling community.

4. *In addressing the need for improved access to higher education, we are missing some simple ways to prevent low-income students from being shut out.* It turns out that more than a third of high school students do not complete the FAFSA in the winter of their senior year. The FAFSA — Free Application for Federal Student Aid — is the only way students can access a wide range of federal financial aid for college, so millions of dollars are left on the table each year. The FAFSA is not only a complicated series of forms, but it requires parents' tax information to complete it, and yet the FAFSA is due months before the April 15 tax deadline, meaning families have to know this and be able to do their taxes early. It's not uncommon, one higher ed expert told me, for low-income students to get into a good school, only to find out in the summer before college starts that they missed all aid deadlines and can't go. Relatively simple solutions could include setting up a system to ensure every public high school student completes the forms at school (just in case they decide to attend college), and/or moving up the timeline when free tax assistance is provided to low-income families, so that those same programs can assist families in completing the FAFSA.

Chapter 2
KEEPING IT REAL

I am no longer willing to accept the things I cannot change.
I am going to change the things I cannot accept.
~ANGELA DAVIS

The happenings of daily life provide me with tools for social change, and social change tools in turn affect my daily life, such as improving my ability to parent. The most overt example of this interconnection came from my friend Anita when she introduced to me the phrase "What does that look like?"

Anita is a therapist, working with individuals and pairs. When a couple is having difficulties in their relationship, but wants to stay together, she often asks a simple question, suggesting the couple make it real for each other: "What does that look like?" A wife may say she doesn't feel respected or a husband might say he doesn't feel loved. What does it look like to be loved? What does it look like to be respected?

Anita finds out pretty quickly what it looks like to be dumbfounded, when each responds dismissively, "Everyone knows what it looks like to be loved," or "Give me a break; respect is respect." Anita pushes again, "For you, describe what it looks like to be loved." The woman says, "I appreciate that he is a better cook, and so I always do the dishes. I feel loved when he comes up behind me while I'm at the sink, and puts his arms around me. It's those small acts of warmth that I shouldn't have to ask for." She lists a few other things, and he shakes his head, taken aback. "That's all you've been wanting?"

It's his turn, but he's still being flip. "She just doesn't respect me. There's nothing more to say." Anita, gently but firmly, "And that looks like…?" He responds, "She would ask me about my day at least after the kids are in bed; usually by then we've talked about her work. She would offer to cook once a week, since we both put in long hours and we do equal parenting time, but I do all the cooking." He is on a roll now. "When we are with other couples, she wouldn't interrupt what I am saying during a conversation. That is so disrespectful."

He expects his wife to be defensive, but her face reflects confusion. "I didn't know you wanted me to cook once a week. We both laugh that my cooking stinks, but I am happy to offer you a break. And I thought you liked the conversation dynamics, those interruptions, since we both come from these boisterous families where that back-and-forth is a sign that we're on a roll, we're interested. And wait, whoa. You've seemed so stressed about your work lately, especially with our second jobs on the weekends, that I thought you said you didn't want to talk about it."

This first conversation doesn't ensure lifetime harmony, but the exercise helps a couple realize that communication and expressions of love or respect don't come magically — you have to make it real. Be clear about what respect and love mean to you, and what it looks like when they happen.

What's obvious to each of us is often hidden to others, and vice versa.

According to Anita, that question, "What does it look like?" — and the journey on which the question takes the couple — has saved many a marriage. The same question can advance our social justice work.

Whether the cause is re-imagining public housing or transforming our health care system, addressing hunger or reducing crime, we can't assume we know how to make change simply because we know change is necessary. We shouldn't assume that the people working alongside us are in agreement about what progress looks like.

When we ask the right questions, when we make the questions concrete and paint a picture with our answers, the conversation happens at a level that will allow us to begin to think of real solutions to real, and frustratingly complex, problems. We need to be specific about our definition of success — for an organization, a project, a movement, a political campaign. And then we must provide the supports and training — built into the work, not added on as an afterthought — to achieve that vision. Making it real is how we make it possible.

The converse is largely the norm. We often expect people in crucial professions that help people — such as medicine and education — to do things that don't come naturally to them, even if they don't know what it looks like.

Principals are expected to lead schools, and teachers are expected to teach students; that's what they are trained to do. But study after study indicates that the involvement of parents in a child's schooling (both at home and at school) is one of the biggest predictors of student success. Yet teachers and principals and school administrators often have no idea how to engage parents, especially parents who are besieged with the complexities of working multiple jobs, who may not speak English fluently, or who were raised to believe that parents are not supposed to be involved with the school.

Principals and teachers are just supposed to know, magically, what a welcoming school looks like and how to get students' parents involved in supporting their children's education. They don't; why would they? And with already overwhelming workloads, it is untenable to take on even more.

Then, with the rise of charter schools and other options for parents to opt out of district public schools, principals and teachers find out they need to become marketing experts too, getting the word out about their school to parents, working with the media, holding events. Now they are supposed to lead and teach, and be experts at engaging overwhelmed parents, and be marketers.

In Boston, and many other cities, people have come together to develop tools to make this real for schools, to make it work for schools. There are now tools on the web with walk-throughs that schools can do to check off whether they have created an environment that invites or discourages family involvement.

One of the system's strongest and longest-serving principals once said to me, "To be honest, I have no idea how to get parents involved who aren't already showing up for things. And the ones who do show up, well I have no idea what to do with them; they tend to be more economically privileged, so I have to figure out how to use their energy and resources to benefit the whole school and not just their child's classroom."

So while school systems around the country are providing professional development for teachers and principals — and experimenting with strategies such as teachers doing summer home visits to get to know their students' families — we need to frontload parent engagement and school marketing. If the work of parent engagement, communications and marketing, plus customer service, is important to being a successful school principal or teacher, build it into their core training. Don't assume it is easy or intuitive, and don't save this training solely for professional development workshops after a principal or teacher is on the job.

What does it look like? That simple question I learned from Anita can be a game-changer for the students and not just the adults. The elementary school principal for my youngest daughter's school, Ethan d'Ablemont Burnes, used this concept openly and effectively. At the beginning of one school year, I watched as he gathered all the kids and parents into a gigantic circle in front of the building. He asked for a student to offer up one of the school mottos. A perky third grader raised his hand to exclaim, "Do your best!"

THAT SIMPLE QUESTION I LEARNED FROM ANITA CAN BE A GAME-CHANGER. I HAVE COME TO THINK OF THIS AS *WILLPOWER*: THE POWER OF WHAT IT LOOKS LIKE.

Next, Ethan said, "Give me an example of what it looks like when a student does his best." The boy responded, "Always check your work when you are done." The principal continued in this way with the remaining components of the school motto, and after each section of the motto — be safe, own what you do, be respectful — he had a student describe what that might look like during a school day. The responses got posted in the hallway for everyone to read throughout the year. Making it real makes it possible.

I think about this with the new and crucial emphasis on DEI — diversity, equity, and inclusion. We've got to make those words come alive. What is diversity? What does equity look like? What is inclusion? And how do they differ from one another? For many, diversity only refers to race and to hiring more people of color, but as we expand our thinking, we are seeing that the most effective companies and organizations bring to the table the contributions of people of all genders, different races, multiple cultures, and more. DEI also means being conscious not just of recruitment and hiring practices but of orientation and retention practices and how a workplace operates overall as a team. Inclusion in particular is one to unpack. In organizations, I've found that to some people it means everyone has a say in all decisions. That is reasonable in a collective, and it was fascinating to me to work in a 10-person collective right out of college, but it is not tenable or appropriate in most workplaces. We must continue to explore what equity and inclusion look like.

In many of our social justice practices, we must ask ourselves, what does that look like? A long-established tenet of voter outreach and community organizing is that it takes at least three contacts (and some argue it takes five to seven contacts) to convince someone to do something they might not otherwise consider, such as vote for a particular candidate or even try a certain product. Before the most important events of the year, such as a school-wide curriculum meeting or one-on-one parent-teacher conferences, school administrators who employ this tenet of three points of contact have the most positive effect on parental turnout. Every family is different, but parents often have busy and overwhelming lives. They can care deeply about their kids, but may not know how to be involved in the school, not have the time, or not feel welcome. Contact One: the classroom teacher sends home in the child's backpack an announcement of the important upcoming meeting. Contact Two: an email or text reminder. Contact Three: a reminder call in the parent's native language. Sound like too much time and effort? It will add hours of regained learning time for a child if her parent or other guardian is further engaged in her learning and can tell the teacher what challenges are going on at home.

During my time working for the mayor, I learned from a fascinating hospital collaboration that looked at the intersection between the arenas of education, health, and housing, using this concept of making it real.

In January 2013, I attended a lively meeting of the advisory board for Boston Children's Hospital, including doctors, nurses, social workers, hospital administrators, representatives of local social service agencies, and representatives of neighborhood groups. I was there representing the mayor. The 15 of us met quarterly to advise the hospital leadership on community needs and on best places for investing the hospital's legally mandated community benefits dollars.

At this particular meeting, two community members made it real for the rest of us how housing and neighborhood development are health care issues. Both women are tireless advocates living in Mission Hill, a Boston neighborhood right near Children's Hospital, with a long and complex history. It once was comprised primarily of moderate and middle-income families, then became a place that struggled with deteriorating conditions and drug use, and is now a mixed community that includes many college students. It was not considered a "good" area of the city until the families living there worked mightily, for years and years, to clean it up, get rid of drug dealers and other crime, beautify the streets and storefronts. But once that happened, and it became more desirable, college students started moving in, which was not the positive you might expect, and not only because rental prices soared.

> AT A PARTICULAR MEETING TWO COMMUNITY MEMBERS MADE IT REAL HOW HOUSING AND NEIGHBORHOOD DEVELOPMENT ARE ALSO HEALTH ISSUES.

Without vilifying college kids as a whole, it is worth noting that many students keep different hours — and have a different lifestyle — than families with children. Imagine this, the two women at the meeting shared with us: You can no longer put your toddlers or school-age children to sleep at 7 or 8 p.m., with any certainty of a good night's sleep, even on a weekday, because of the noise from the college students. The police will only respond if it is after 11 p.m., long after your young children need to be asleep. When you go outside in the morning on Sundays, your lawn reeks from students who got drunk the night before and peed or even puked in front of your house. Trash is on the street from students who dropped it on the way to the dumpster, drawing rodents. So when you go to push your toddler in the stroller on the way to childcare, your child screams, coming eye-level with a large rat. Rats become more and more common, their droppings everywhere. Now imagine what that neighborhood looks like, feels like, smells like, from that child's eye level. And imagine what she is breathing, as you are trying to manage your child's asthma. On very little sleep.

The women representing this neighborhood made it real for us. At the meeting we agreed that universities need to recognize that they are located in a neighborhood where non-students live. And they must make that reality clear to their students: We share this community with people of all ages, including families with children and the elderly. If you choose to live off-campus, in an apartment or house, you must respect their health and safety and peace. Do not play loud music after 8 p.m. Place trash in secure receptacles. It should go without saying: Do not use people's yards as if they were bathrooms.

When we ask the right questions and we focus on what progress actually looks like, we significantly amp up our ability to make change. So now, at the beginning of many projects, especially when the people gathered in the room have too much already on their plates, and we are going to be asking them to do even more, I say, "I want you to think of what success for this work would look like in this way: What — very specifically — needs to happen within the next year so that this effort will have been worth your time? What does success look like to you?" I have come to think of this as WILLpower: the power of What It Looks Like.

What does privilege look like? What does it look like to live without privilege and have to compete against those who take it for granted? This is a potent topic right now, as we try to expand the conversation on racial and economic inequities to audiences who don't think these are a problem anymore in the US. My brother Jeff (the teacher I told you about) shared a video with me. An instructor in a college program holds out a $100 bill, as a few dozen young adults line up in gym clothes at the start of a race. He says the winner of the race gets the $100. Before the race begins, however, he wants people to take two large steps forward if they can answer yes to each question. Take two steps forward if you had access to a private education. "Take two steps forward," he adds, "if you had access to a free tutor growing up." Then, "Take two steps forward if you never had to help mom or dad with the bills. Take two steps forward if you don't have to help pay for your college education. Take two steps forward if you never wondered where your next meal was going to come from." He notes that the people now starting the race 20 feet back might still be able to win, but is this a fair race? And if the people who start 20 feet ahead win it, how will they know if they won on their merits or from the head start someone else gave them?

For my job, I have read the research showing that by the time the kids of middle- and upper-income families turn 12, they have had an average of 6,000 more hours of time to learn outside the classroom than their peers from low-income and poor families. Now *that* makes it real what kids are up against.

This concept of making it real has helped me outside the social justice realm, as a mom. A man I met told me about his work to address distracted driving. When my eldest was training for her driver's license, I had already tried to make it real that she is not just driving a car; she is operating a 3,000-pound machine that can kill those in and outside the vehicle. I knew she was likely tuning me out.

So this safety advocate shook up my own thinking with his explanation to bring alive the term "distracted driving": Where do you want your attention to be when a small child darts in front of your car?

I repeated to my daughter a few times, "Where do you want your attention to be when a small child darts in front of your car — on the road or looking down at your phone?" I then made a solution real, requiring that anytime my daughter was going to get behind the wheel, her phone had to be placed in the seat behind her where she could not reach it, so she simply could not pick up a call or check a text.

Better yet was when I modeled for her, as I drove: "My phone's ringing. I'm going to pull over and see if it's important," or "It's hard to ignore that urgent sound of a text coming in. I'm going to turn off my phone for this car ride. I can check messages when we get to the market."

I noticed my daughter noticing my habits. Then once I realized I myself was falling prey to the addictive ringtone of the phone a few years later, I put a sign in the back window of my car: "Save a life. Focus on the road, not your phone." While drivers behind me often honked their approval, what they didn't know was that I placed it right where I would see the message when I looked into the rear view mirror — reminding myself of the safe thing to do.

Making it real is essential in the fight against global warming and in components of that effort, such as promoting fewer cars and more bikes. According to the League of American Bicyclists, bike use has risen over 60 percent since 2000. If we want to make it safer for people to ride bikes in cities, not only do we need to expand the numbers of bike lanes, but we should also advocate that state departments of motor vehicles include bicycle awareness in driver's ed courses and in the requirements for renewing our licenses. What does it look like to safely share the road with bicycles? We can't assume that drivers know. As with principal and teacher training that builds in classes on parent engagement, or medical schools that require courses on bedside manner, if it's important enough, build it into the training. Make it real.

> MAKING IT REAL, DEFINING SUCCESS, TURNS THE OVERWHELMING INTO THE POSSIBLE.

Making it real, defining success, turns the overwhelming into the possible. Another time this hit home for me was as a daughter of an aging parent. I was 55 and my mom was 84, battling a kind of cancer called multiple myeloma, when I read a brilliant book.

In *Being Mortal: Medicine and What Matters* in the End, physician Atul Gawande tackles the complex question of how we can help our loved ones (and ourselves) be clear about what kind of death we want, not just what kind of life we want, specifically how to avoid having medical options and interventions define our final days. Gawande makes real what a better relationship looks like between a doctor and their dying patient, understanding that most patients will opt for extreme intervention in the hopes their life can be saved, even when those interventions are unlikely to succeed, likely to cause additional pain and suffering, and might even shorten rather than lengthen survival. Ask real questions, such as:

1. Do you want to be resuscitated if your heart stops?
2. Do you want aggressive treatments such as intubation and mechanical ventilation?
3. Do you want tube or intravenous feeding if you can't eat on your own?

Researchers found not just that this list of questions ensured a patient's providers and family knew her wishes, but, more important, the existence of the form with these questions ensured that crucial end of life and quality of life conversations could take place. It made the painful and difficult into the possible.

Gawande found that Swedish doctors call these "breakpoint discussions." Often the conversations result in less intervention and a more peaceful death, when near-term death is inevitable. Sometimes the results are different. Through one of those conversations, a colleague of Gawande's learned that her terminally ill father, who had advanced cancer, did in fact want more intervention than she would have expected. He was a professor and she expected that intellectual stimulation and a certain level of academic output might be what he required to want to stay alive. Instead she learned that at this stage of his life, for him a quality life meant being able to eat chocolate ice cream and watch football on TV. That would be enough to warrant intervention and lengthen his life.

As my mom ended her initial six months of chemotherapy, the cancer went into remission, and she was preparing to meet with her doctor, who had been urging her to continue with a lower dose of maintenance chemo to keep the cancer at bay. As a result of Gawande's book, I was able to ask her to define a quality of life and whether it was chocolate ice cream and football. She was pensive and then clear; for her, quality meant:

- Having the ability to take walks outdoors, not being so weak from the medication side effects that she could only meander the hallways.
- Having a mind clear enough to play bridge with her friends and read novels, not fuzzy from the medication.

- Being independent enough to do some basic errands on her own, not constantly having gastric pain and a lack of ability to control her bladder.
- Helping others, whether it be her library volunteering or serving as the welcome wagon for elders entering her community.

We sent this information to her doctor, and, in a pleasant surprise, when we met with him, he stopped pressuring her to continue the chemo. He finally understood that the medication, and the additional medication to ameliorate the side effects of the original medication, was limiting her quality of life. Within three months of ceasing treatment, she was back to doing everything on her list! She knew the cancer might eventually (or soon) kill her, but she was clear she'd rather live a quality life than have more years.

During the COVID-19 pandemic, it certainly helped all of us understand the importance of "social distancing" when public health experts made it real; they issued charts that illustrated the trajectory of the disease with and without "sheltering in place." A key step in making the necessary steps real, addressing the concern that the epidemic was being blown out of proportion, was when those experts clarified that social distancing was not just for individuals to remain healthy, but to slow the disease spread so that it would not overwhelm the healthcare system (leaving them without enough respirators and thus having to choose to let some patients die), and that healthy individuals spreading the disease to others (particularly the elderly and immune-compromised) was a huge factor in stemming the pandemic.

I appreciated the reminder, in the early days of the pandemic, that if the disease did not kill millions of people, and if it were to blow over relatively quickly, it wouldn't mean that the early warnings were wrong, but that the steps taken as a result of those early warnings were successful.

This social media post made it real why emptying the streets was an act of global unity:

When you go out and see the empty streets, the empty stadiums, the empty train platforms, don't say to yourself, "My God, it looks like the end of the world." What you're seeing is love in action.

What you're seeing, in that negative space, is how much we do care for each other, for our grandparents, for our immuno-compromised brothers and sisters, for people we will never meet.

People will lose jobs over this. Some will lose their businesses. And some will lose their lives. All the more reason to take a moment, when you're out on your walk, or on your way to the store, or just watching the news, to look into the emptiness and marvel at all of that love. Let it fill you and sustain you. It isn't the end of the world. It is the most remarkable act of global solidarity we may ever witness. It is the reason the world will go on.

Making it real includes setting specific and measurable goals. We have known for a number of years that teenagers facing multiple life stresses are more likely to make it through high school if they have a strong mentor relationship with at least one adult in the building. That connection provides a safety net as students jump the hurdles of school. So what does a good high school look like? One standard should be that by the time they graduate, every student in that school is so well known by at least one adult in the school that the adult can write a detailed, double-spaced, two-page college letter of recommendation about the student. We're talking an absolute minimum standard here, but not every high school offers even this step, which makes real what high school reform looks like when it is based on what we know about students, families, and schools.

In our political movements, we need to use various means to drive home a point, either to make a potential solution real or, sometimes, to simply highlight the problem. This quote on the environment circulates on social media: "We are living on this planet as if we had another one to go to." This is unfortunately true for individuals, but more troubling, it is true for our systems: large scale practices of industries and national government policies.

Often, in making it real, the stakes for me have been high. In 2008, Mayor Menino and United Way unveiled the initiative "Thrive in 5: Boston's Promise to its Children," a roadmap toward universal school readiness. It aimed to bridge the learning gap already evident when low-income and poor children reach the kindergarten classroom, a gap that simply widens if not caught early. After the initiative was announced and early work undertaken, in 2010, we received a rare $1.5 million two-year grant from the Kellogg Foundation.

But in the winter of 2012, I was dismayed to learn that we were unlikely to receive a renewal of this grant that was making such a difference in Boston — and I knew we needed more time to build the changes into the fabric of the city.

The goal of Thrive in 5 was to significantly interrupt the cycles of poverty and family isolation that play a huge role in children's educational underachievement, hobbling their futures. We had used Kellogg's initial investment to organize parents to educate other parents about the importance of the first five years of life, and to improve access to free services and activities to reach isolated mothers (isolated due to domestic violence, depression, or other significant life issues).

A small team of us had wrestled for two years to land that initial grant, with me representing the mayor, so the potential non-renewal hit me hard. Joelle Jude Fontaine, the program officer who gave me the warning news, admitted that the structure of her last site visit to Boston had not impressed her or her colleagues. She described meetings that were vague and formal, no true sense of what the work meant to Boston. I convinced her to come back, since much had changed in the intervening six months. While delegating to and developing others should always be paramount, this time, with so much money at stake, I decided I'd better run (okay, I'll admit I decided to *micromanage*) the site visit.

For three full days, Peg Sprague (the lead person at United Way for this project) and I attached ourselves at the hip to the three-person Kellogg team. We picked them up in my aging silver minivan at their hotel first thing in the morning, ferried them around all day from project to

project, and dropped them back off after dinner. Sure, we had the oblig-
atory policy meetings with city and state officials, but we also took them
to see what was happening with parents in a number of neighborhoods.
They witnessed our play-to-learn groups for parents, grandparents, and
guardians of children under age three, located in the public schools. These
groups bring parents together, making sure young kids get a chance to interact with other kids and experience the joy of learning, while introducing parents (many of whom are immigrants) to schools where they might
send their kids at age five.

I couldn't have planned one interaction better: A quiet woman
dressed in jeans and a sweatshirt with a baby in her arms walked up to
Joelle, the Kellogg program officer, and said, "I hear you help pay for this
program and I can't thank you enough. I was really depressed after my first
child was born, and then got diagnosed with breast cancer. I considered
hurting myself and I considered giving away my baby. When someone
brought me to this group, I made friends, I learned where to get help for
depression, and I finally found some joy in being with my kid. She is now
in kindergarten in this school — and this here is my second baby! I don't
know where I'd be without this program, so now I spend a couple hours a
week doing outreach to get other parents to come here too."

Over lunch that day, Peg and I explained to the Kellogg team the
creative ways we were building alliances across sectors (higher ed, health
care, public schools, etc.) to support parents of young kids, and being
more concrete in our practices, again illustrating the real ways their grant
was working. Even those most isolated parents (who might reject any social services out of fear of being deported or located by an abusive ex-boy-
friend) usually still take their children to the doctor and tend to trust their
doctor more than anyone else. We brought physicians at our health centers into the early childhood activity plan; they had begun writing "pre-
scriptions" for parents to bring their kids to these play-to-learn groups, as
important as any other medicine for children who weren't socializing with
others.

After lunch, Peg, the Kellogg team, and I traveled across town to see
a large greenhouse where low-income parents and young kids are learning
to grow their own food. In that same neighborhood, they met a Cape

Verdean grocery store owner who has her own radio show, geared to Cape Verdean families. Information she learned about early brain development from our Kellogg-funded Thrive in 5 initiative so inspired her that she began sharing it on her radio show, and she now invites parents to come in to her market and learn about neighborhood school readiness programming. This is what was changing in the city as a result of the Kellogg investment.

We made it real: all three days, Joelle and her colleagues met people at our health centers and on the streets, in the libraries and in the schools, parents and social service providers for whom this initiative had changed their work and their lives.

The conversations, meals, and meetings were interesting to the Kellogg team, but it was clear that what swayed them was seeing the initiative in action: the parents and children at the playgroups; watching a Vietnamese outreach worker talk to other pregnant women at an ice cream shop; seeing the Cape Verdean shop owner display materials in her store window, in Creole, illustrating how parents can talk, read, and play with their newborns. These interactions made real all the information we put in our written reports. We hoped to convince Kellogg at least to be proud of what their investments had accomplished, and ideally to fund us further.

Back in Michigan three weeks later, Joelle called to say we would receive another $1.2 million! Her board had not been initially receptive to continued funding in Boston, since other areas of the country were a higher priority for them. We had made it real for Joelle, and she returned to her office and went to bat for Boston. She thanked us for showing what a city can do, and said she was hopeful we would improve our ability to measure success and then share the lessons with other parts of the country.

As is often true in our justice work, to turn the difficult into the possible, we need WILLpower — the potency of what it looks like.

Chapter 3
POWER

A developed country is not a place where the poor have cars.
It's where the rich use public transportation.
~ENRIQUE PENALOSA, MAYOR OF
BOGOTÁ, COLOMBIA

Wouldn't it be grand if our social justice choices weren't complicated or painful? Stumbling down a rocky path, you come to a fork in the road. Which way to go? Bringing your heels together three times, eyes closed, you chant, "I want to do the right thing, I want to do the right thing. . . " A glowing Good Witch appears, her jeweled wand pointing to the sunlit justice-brick-road.

Too often fog surrounds us, neither path nor guide in sight. My mother introduced this concept to me early in life: We each have power, but it's not always easy to determine how to use it.

When my parents split up, Mom and I moved to a small apartment in San Francisco. My oldest brother, Mike, trekked off to college across the country, and middle brother Jeff went to live with Dad (swearing to make life hell for him and his new wife, which I hear he did). Things were rocky, financially. Mom and I settled into the second floor of a small building on a street of pink and gray stucco apartments, next to the N streetcar tracks, at 34th and Judah.

It was, surprisingly, a good point in my life's journey. When I saw my dad, we took walks or went out for a meal. At a point when many teens were battling with their parents, Mom and I fell into a pleasant routine, each largely doing our own thing. She decreed we should take the phone off the hook for an hour of quiet each night, so we talked over dinner. Mom experimented with healthy meals; I had clean-up and laundry duty, pulling a small metal cart to the nearby laundromat. She mopped, and I vacuumed. Mom worked full-time as a bookkeeper, and I was independent getting to school via San Francisco buses. I landed my first job, cleaning the house of an elderly man next door.

MY MOTHER INTRODUCED THIS CONCEPT TO ME EARLY IN LIFE: WE EACH HAVE POWER, BUT IT'S NOT ALWAYS EASY TO DETERMINE HOW TO USE IT.

Somehow, though, only troubled families moved in downstairs. I didn't mind at all when I was 14 and the kind lady arrived with her gorgeous, bad-boy 16-year-old who flirted with me shamelessly. Hard to hide my disappointment when they left six months later.

In moved another mom, this time with two toddlers. So much yelling came from the apartment. One day, when I was in ninth grade, after school I heard what sounded like hitting, and then a child sobbing. Then quiet. I sat down on the floor and put my ear right up to the vent, heart pounding.

I called mom at work and asked what to do. She laid it out: "You don't know for sure, since you didn't see anything. You could call the police, but there are some risks, honey, if the mother is in fact hitting her kids. One is that the authorities will investigate and not have enough evidence to take action, and she might take out her anger and embarrassment on the children. On the other hand, these children might be getting hurt, and we might be able to get them help. Unless you tell me you hear this escalating, I am going to let you decide."

I thought about it, as I opened and closed the phone book, eventually placing an anonymous tip. (In 1976, there was no such thing as Caller ID.) The agency rep did ask for my name, but when I refused, she still took the information and thanked me for calling.

Nothing for a few days. I remember purposely staying late at school, not wanting to arrive home before Mom. Then one night our phone rang. It was the downstairs woman. Furious that some officials had come knocking on her door, with a few threatening words she asked if we had called about her. I remember her tone, and my unease, but not what she said. Frightened, I insisted no, it wasn't us, said I had no idea what she was talking about.

The children stayed put. The family moved out the next month. We never saw them again. I had to ask myself: Did I help or hurt? Did I use my power for good?

I like that dictionaries boast several definitions for "power":
* *the ability to act or produce an effect*
* *possession of control, authority, or influence over others*
* *mental or moral efficacy*
* *physical might*
* *a source or means of supplying energy*

Reflecting on my life and my work, it's clear that while people are born into different circumstances that provide different levels of opportunity, we all have some kinds of power, and the key is identifying our power and being intentional about how to use it.

There are those who have more overt power — power over others, often in positions of some kind of leadership. When someone gains power over others, whether as the corporate CEO or police officer, judge or college professor or governor, it does change people, doesn't it? And it changes the people who surround those in power. How can we be wise with our power; that is, how can we be intentional? How do we remain a mission-focused, good person, the person we want to be, while wielding power? To paraphrase Winston Churchill, with great power comes great responsibility.

I think often about what I call *daily* or *personal* power to interrupt injustice and make a stand when it matters, or sometimes simply to help. Sometimes we can exert our power and make a difference. Maybe occasionally our efforts make things worse. Other times, as in my attempt to help the kids who lived below us in San Francisco, we do what we can, with no obvious results.

The power I saw and used when working for the Boston mayor was a more institutionalized form of power, one that could affect communities or the entire city. And there were also times when I used my personal power to influence the mayor's *positional* power, like when I made same-sex couples with children real for him.

Tom Menino, a Boston native, was elected to his first of five four-year terms as mayor in 1993. I started working for him a few years after he was elected the first time, and soon learned that Boston City Hall is more than merely a building; it's an institution.

Working for Mayor Menino, being inside City Hall, was a very different experience from what I'd anticipated. It established my belief in government as a safeguard and safety net, as a provider of services for the common well-being, as a power for good.

I didn't start the job with that perspective, however. I was 34 when I arrived at Boston City Hall. And while I hoped working for the city would effectively bring positive change to local communities, I was ignorant about those who worked for the government. I assumed that maybe 40 percent of the people in government would turn out to be extraordinarily talented and dedicated and the rest might be tired longtime civil servants or people with few skills who were hired merely due to personal connections. Why so cynical? I grew up in the post-Watergate era, when most of us viewed government cynically, assuming those with power abused it to make inappropriate hires — nepotism and other kinds of patronage — and all kinds of unethical choices.

I found the opposite to be true. The overwhelming majority of people I worked with in Boston City Hall, right from the start, were talented, hard-working, and, as we say in Boston, wicked smart. From what I could tell over all the years I was there, the small percentage of people hired solely as a result of connections or favors, and the percentage of people doing mediocre work, was no different than in the private sector.

My cubicle sat inside the Mayor's Office of Neighborhood Services, where young professionals served as Mayor Menino's liaisons, his eyes and ears to each neighborhood and to each cultural community in the vastly diverse city: the East Boston Coordinator, the Jamaica Plain Coordinator, the Vietnamese Coordinator, the Latino Coordinator.

From the cabinet chiefs to the line staff, the people in City Hall inspired me, whether they were taking care of daily business (birth certificates, marriage licenses, snow removal) or revamping the city's schools; whether attracting federal money to rebuild safer low-cost housing, or teaching kids growing up in poverty how to swim at our community centers. I observed staff members devoting long hours, working on personal, individual

FROM THE CABINET CHIEFS TO THE LINE STAFF, THE PEOPLE IN CITY HALL INSPIRED ME, WHETHER THEY WERE TAKING CARE OF DAILY BUSINESS (BIRTH CERTIFICATES, MARRIAGE LICENSES, SNOW REMOVAL) OR REVAMPING THE CITY'S SCHOOLS ...

levels: making sure repair teams got out to fix streetlights knocked out in a storm; helping a family find childcare; explaining the process to residents for putting an addition onto their home; supporting the development of local crime watch groups. I heard them respond with patience and respect to furious phone calls from residents who blamed them and the mayor for everything that nature threw their way, with rarely a thank you for finding housing for dozens of families left homeless by a random fire or severe storm. I heard these staff members handle virtually every call with aplomb, then hang up to vent to their colleagues and occasionally cry from the stress of the job.

I saw this dedication throughout my 17 years working for the mayor. The week of one of Boston's largest snowstorms, in February of 2013, many of his staffers slept in their office to respond to emergencies. Two months later, in April, a pair of brothers set off bombs at the Boston Marathon finish line, killing three people and injuring hundreds more. Virtually every City Hall employee volunteered, on no sleep, to staff the mayor's 24-hour hotline, as well as to house and feed marathoners who couldn't get home. For weeks after, the mayor's liaisons met with every small business affected by the bombs, helping each one complete insurance paperwork, organizing grief counselors for their employees.

Not long after the mayor hired me, I noted that of the staff close to him, many were there because of a personal commitment to the man, an interest in running for office themselves eventually, or both. While I wasn't surprised by these motivations, I found myself struggling to figure out my place, as I didn't fall into those categories. I was much more interested in *policy* than *politics*. I came to work in City Hall with no personal relationship to the mayor and no interest in running for elected office.

I met Tom Menino when I was managing Allston-Brighton Healthy Boston, a neighborhood coalition of health and human service providers and businesses. In that role, I moderated a 1993 debate among the 13 mayoral candidates, of which he was one. Two years after he won office for the first time, Mayor Menino called me to meet with him, having seen my work in the debate and after. It was such an important moment in my career that I can remember exactly what I wore to the meeting, where he and I sat down to talk in his office overlooking bustling Faneuil Hall marketplace. It was a black silk short-sleeved blouse tucked into a gray skirt that was professional, but with a busy pattern of roses that I felt allowed me to express some of my playful side.

The mayor said he wanted to bring to City Hall more people with fresh perspectives on government, folks who had been successful in other settings at bringing people together across opposing viewpoints, developing new programs, raising money. He teased, "How again did you get that huge grant from me to launch the immigrant leadership program in Allston-Brighton?!"

Sitting in his office chatting, Tom Menino was charming and convincing, telling me he was open to creating a new position for me to come work with him on education, health, and human services. I asked for a few weeks to consider his offer, and he said he'd call for an answer one month later. I'll never forget the phone ringing at dinnertime on the designated day, shushing my kids playing in the background, his firm voice: "Laurie, Tom Menino here. What's your decision?"

My personality is fairly confident, and my demeanor largely extroverted, but these characteristics obscure an inherent shyness. I didn't know many people when I came on board, and I rarely did the going-out-for-drinks-after-work thing, which was interpreted by some in City Hall as me being aloof. Thus, I lacked a type of power, that of being in the inner circles. But my role as something of an outsider also gave me power — I didn't worry about upsetting the mayor or seeming disloyal by raising new issues or by questioning a decision. There wasn't a friendship to protect.

The mayor was supportive and respectful of my work, asking me to develop programs and policies that cut across the silos of education, health, and human services, and I loved meeting with him.

Just twice, Mayor Menino shared areas of deep personal ambivalence with me, and each time I used whatever power I had to encourage him to think differently.

The first time it had to do with marriage equality. In 2004, I had a woman partner; together we were raising three young kids. I was chatting about same-sex marriage with one of Mayor Menino's long-time aides. I asked whether the mayor had taken a stand on marriage versus civil unions. The aide said he had not and that most likely the farthest the mayor would go would be to openly support civil unions. I knew I would be getting questions from community members about his stance as the marriage equality debate heated up, especially as opponents mobilized to change the Massachusetts constitution to ban such unions.

During my next meeting with the mayor about something unrelated, I casually asked where he stood. He explained, "I support civil unions, but Laurie, you gotta understand, I am not gonna be comfortable with gay marriage. Some of my best friends are gay couples who've been together a long time, but I grew up Catholic…." Then we talked about my kids and his grandkids, the younger generations being his soft spot. I shared my concern that the children of same-sex couples were going to bear the brunt of their parents not obtaining full legal rights. It worried me that if the Massachusetts constitution were amended to ban same-sex marriage, it would be the only instance I could think of where we would be ensuring kids' parents couldn't marry, that we'd be intentionally creating a permanent class of "bastards." As his brow furrowed at that concept, I saw an opening. I mentioned that people often forget marriage creates not just rights, but *responsibilities*, protections for the adults and for the kids.

We talked for a bit, and he asked more about my children. He had met them many times, both at community events and when they came in to City Hall with me (looking for the M&Ms the mayor famously kept in a glass jar on his desk). As I left, I asked, "Sir, you don't mind if I raise this issue from time to time, do you?" He laughed, shook his head, and said I should go right ahead, before firmly booting me out to make time for the next staff member. I shamelessly dropped by his office with my kids (then ages 9, 6, and 2, and pretty darn cute) a few extra times in the following weeks.

On February 29, 2004, one month after our talk, I opened the newspaper and received a shock. *Boston Globe* writer Michael Jonas titled his column "For Mayor, Gay Rights are Simply Civil Rights." His piece opened with "If gay marriage has become the battleground of the culture wars in America, someone forgot to tell Tom Menino. Menino evinces little hesitation at embracing the expansion of marriage rights to same-sex couples…. For Hizzoner, it's less about grand theories of human nature than it is about the human-scale-realities encountered every day in a city." Jonas quoted the mayor, "I have some folks who work for me who are gay and have kids. They nurture those kids; they cherish those kids. Some other folks who are heterosexual don't do enough for their kids."

I rushed in to the mayor's office that morning and, without thinking about it, embraced him, stepping back afterwards, embarrassed by my own effusiveness (as his assistants Annette and Marguerite looked at me sternly). I blurted out, "Thank you for what you said to Michael Jonas." His reply: "You know, kiddo, I was talking about you and your kids." I had made LGBT families and marriage equality real for him, through personal power.

After Mayor Menino went on the record in the *Boston Globe* supporting marriage equality, he continued to wear that mantle, locally and nationally. When the first same-sex marriage licenses in the US were to be issued in Massachusetts on May 17, 2004, he announced that all senior staff in City Hall were free to take the day off from our normal duties and serve as greeters for arriving couples, or help deal with the protesters out front.

I know that one series of conversations with one staff member doesn't make the man. Taking a brave stand on controversial issues was not new for Tom Menino. He had already done so on many issues — such as providing clean needles for addicts as they struggled with recovery — long before others. To him these weren't even brave or bold actions, just necessary. That was the power of this particular man: When he did the right thing, he did it with little fanfare, because he honestly thought discrimination and fear of difference were just plain stupid, and he said so.

So it certainly wasn't all about my conversations with the mayor, but

I used my power, which meant taking a risk. Because, you see, there's a little more to the story. The aide I originally questioned about the mayor's stance on civil unions asked me *not* to bring up marriage with the mayor. He reminded me that Menino had been a long-time LGBT rights supporter — all the way back to his time as a city councilor — and had gone out on all kinds of limbs, like single-handedly passing an executive order to grant health insurance coverage to same-sex partners of city employees. He asked that I not bother or pressure the mayor. He said we didn't want to seem ungrateful for his support and this was not the time to push him harder. I said okay, but then thought about it and ignored his request. My instinct told me the mayor would appreciate me using quiet power to raise a topic with him, especially if the issue was one that resonated with his deep beliefs.

I learned early on that some of the people surrounding the mayor came to feel their job was to protect him and not upset him, given the stress of his 24/7/365 schedule. It was their way of expressing loyalty, and I understand that. It often happens with people working closely with someone in power. In politics, but in other settings too, those staffing a leader can feel like caretakers, wary of how any and every slight misstep can make the news, and protective of the health of leaders who work tirelessly, endlessly.

When someone closer to the mayor than me asked me not to bother him, I did often defer. Sometimes I did so because I agreed with them or figured they knew more than I did, and sometimes because I feared being considered disloyal.

Curious about the question of loyalty, and its relationship to power, I have spoken with elected leaders on the state and national stage, as well as corporate and foundation leaders. I've wanted to understand this problematic dynamic of people in inner circles who eventually grow to feel their job is to protect, not challenge (or even fully inform), their boss. When asked to stop and think about it, most leaders admit the problem is a combination of how they handle themselves (do they really make it known to staff that a challenge is welcome?) and how their staff begin to see their own jobs. As with the importance of naming an issue, one leader told me the first step is simply for him and others like him to be conscious of how often they end up surrounded by people who believe their job is to follow versus inform.

Anyone who finds themselves in a position of this kind of power in the public or private sector must hire people who understand that their job *is* to "bother" the boss. Part of Mayor Menino's success came from making sure not to surround himself with yes-people. His Chief Operating Officer, Dennis DiMarzio, taught me to question what was going on if someone who reported to me, or who was vying for a consulting position, seemed to agree with me too much; Dennis taught me to notice the difference between the person having a good idea that resonated with me (a good thing), versus the person rephrasing something I myself had said, as a way of flattering me.

If you are assuming a position of power in any setting, I'd urge you to be clear what your strengths and weaknesses are, and hire senior staff whose strengths counterbalance your weaknesses, staff who look at situations and people very differently from the way you do. And then be explicit with your hires: *If you agree with me all the time, I will assume you aren't doing your homework or you are kissing up, and I will let you go.* Leaders then need to ask themselves continuously: What am I doing to discourage my staff from challenging me? What definition of loyalty am I conveying? I remember a confidential conversation on this topic with a former presidential candidate who told me that when he served in elected office, he had to rely on his wife — smart, perceptive, and honest — to tell him the real deal; staff members often shied away from the truth he needed. Reflecting back, he said he wasn't sure what he did that made his own top staff be so protective.

It isn't easy for people in power to remember that the right kind of leaders don't create followers; they create more leaders.

While I am talking here about people in positions of grand and overt power, the concepts are true far beyond the world of politics. Power in personal relationships. Power at work. As I write this, I am the second-in-command to the CEO of a nonprofit which is modest in size ($8 million budget) and powerful in educational impact (part of the Outward

Bound network). I frequently have to decide when to weigh in, when to be silent, not out of hesitation but to give my boss the room to manage on his own. I have to decide when to push gently and when to push hard. What I saw and learned and tried in the world of government helps guide me about how to be direct, sometimes using playfulness. In mid-2017 I was wrestling with how brilliant and creative my boss was, because it sometimes meant he wasn't disciplined with how to use his time and how he and I should divvy up the work. So I took a breath and said, "You are a force of nature, and sometimes I am not sure when, how, and whether to try to rein you in!" Almost without fail in my career, as happened that day, I found my boss appreciative of this kind of honesty.

How did I myself manage the inherent power that came from working in the mayor's office and thus representing him outside City Hall? I indeed used it, but I felt strongly I wouldn't do so for personal gain. Notably, I saw the same ethic in my City Hall colleagues. For example, I had the power to contact almost anyone at any level in any organization or corporation and get an immediate return call. The mayor's office was phoning! Because I used those calls to engage a person or company in an effort to improve the quality of life for our residents, I had no ambivalence about that access. One time that meant it only took a week to get every hospital head of ob-gyn in the city into one room to talk with the mayor about the problem of rising infant mortality rates.

When using my power *within* City Hall, my standard was not to ask anything of anyone I wouldn't be willing to do myself and not to ask for something to be done for *anyone* without reminding the person that it ought to be done for *everyone*. When my neighbors across the street were frustrated with the molasses pace of getting an addition approved for their house from the city's zoning authorities, they showed me how they had followed all the protocols, proof that their application was languishing. When I spoke with the person in charge at City Hall, I asked about their case but also asked for accountability about their red tape. What could he do about all applicants in the same circumstance?

Tom Menino was a positive role model to me as an individual in power. He passed away from cancer at age 71 in 2014, and some pundits rightly noted that it will take time to truly understand how he maintained power for an unprecedented 20 years, leaving behind no scandals. *Boston Globe* columnist Tom Keane wrote just after the mayor's death, "Mayor Menino's success was not merely his love of people; it was his ability to accumulate power, wield it, and put it to good ends."

However, there were certainly people who disagreed with the mayor and felt frozen out of city decisions, and people who had run against him in elections only to find their reputations and connections greatly reduced afterward. The mayor was rumored to have both a temper and an elephant's memory for anyone who crossed him. However, only twice in 17 years did I encounter his temper, and both times it was on a day when he had been working too long and too hard, and had been ill.

I did find that once he thought someone was a star, they rarely fell from grace; and once he decided someone (inside or outside City Hall) was less than impressive, it took a lot to change his mind. For example, he was very upset when Children's Hospital cut a neighborhood program providing dental care for low-income residents. Initially, Mayor Menino had no interest in hearing about the financial challenges of the hospital, the possibility that those services were unsustainable, or other ways the care was being provided. A few of us had to work hard to get the mayor to re-think his conclusion that the hospital no longer could be trusted to serve the community at all. He did come around. Similarly, the mayor once disagreed with a Boston YMCA construction decision and its temporary impact on services for homeless people. It took a lot of work and time to convince him it was worth rebuilding a relationship with the then-president of the Y.

However, when it came down to it, when he was provided with information and advice beyond what he'd previously been told, I found the mayor contemplative and appreciative, not angry or punitive. It also wasn't hard for me to cut him slack, not to expect the perfection people seem to expect of leaders — I certainly didn't rise at 4 a.m. and work until 11 p.m. or later, 6–7 days a week and most days of the calendar year. He lived and breathed his work.

On a simpler level, even with someone whose roots were as humble as Tom Menino's (lifelong Bostonian in a modest neighborhood who only completed college once in elected office), I found myself trying to imagine how I myself might change if everywhere I went, I carried overt power. If people told me how wonderful I was. If I never again needed to find a parking space or make a reservation at a restaurant. Even those small things — how can they not change a person? This kind of self-reflection is crucial if we are to wield power justly.

I learned from Tom Menino. It comforted me to run into the mayor grocery shopping with his wife, Angela, at Roche Brothers supermarket. Many leaders lose touch with the day-to-day realities of the people they are supposed to serve, and we need to call them on it. The mayor didn't lose touch. When we were angling for a national foundation grant and the grant-maker came to town to visit, a hot topic was the price of gas — how the skyrocketing cost was impacting low-income workers who had to commute to their jobs. The mayor said he was equally concerned about the rising cost of bread and milk, and cited the price, from a recent trip to the grocery store. I took in the surprised and impressed look in the funder's eyes.

Mayor Menino, and those of us who worked for him, had a very specific, concentrated, visible kind of power. Daily power, personal power, is something different: it can be the ability to intervene when we see a wrong, to ask the right questions, and to proactively get involved in a cause we care about, even if our time and skills are limited.

So when do we intervene? When do we hold back? Around the time I was reading *Anne Frank*, in third grade, my dad and I went to an amusement park. We heard anguished howling, and turned to see an angry man horribly abusing his dog, slamming the light brown greyhound repeatedly against a chain link fence. Instinctively, I started to pull away from my father to go do something. Grabbing me, Dad insisted that sometimes we can't get involved because it might not be safe. I adored my pop, but he was a big guy and I thought he should have stepped in; it really bothered me.

However, years later, when I was living in San Francisco, one night I played the same role, at age 17, holding back my boyfriend when he wanted to jump in to stop a man who seemed high on drugs and was beating another guy. Someone had already called the police, and I was worried about William's safety. It was a disturbing scene, though, one man slamming the head of the other against the sidewalk, and I felt sick urging William to hold back. It's not always clear how and when to use our daily power.

Two times on the Boston subway, I faced a decision about whether to intervene, about how to use my personal power in situations where I felt someone was being mistreated. Both cases involved people of color, which caused me, a white woman, to hesitate. Even now I wonder: Was I right or wrong? Both incidents stood out to me enough that I journaled about them at the time.

Spring of 2009. I was in a good mood on the way to City Hall, riding the packed orange line subway, when a child began whining and screeching two seats down. He went on and on, testing everyone's patience, this four-year-old, yelling mostly in Spanish, while sitting on his mom's lap. She looked close to crying or hitting him, really both. I asked the man in between us if I could switch with him to try to help out, knowing I was possibly being invasive and foolish. Now sitting next to the screaming boy and visibly stressed mother, I started talking to the kid in English and my limited Spanish. I found out he was arguing that he wanted his mom to buy him an airplane toy, and his mom simply wanted him to be quiet for the trip to his Head Start classroom. She looked sad and said it had been a rough morning. I asked the boy in Spanish where he would fly a plane when he became a pilot someday; he was intrigued, and stopped whining to think.

Instead of telling me to mind my own business, the mom seemed appreciative. She hadn't known about this concept of re-directing — that is, not fighting the same fight over and over with a kid, and not giving in, but redirecting a child's attention, often by asking an unexpected question. I told her I was impressed that she stayed calm and held her son close. I told her the ages of my kids and how often I lost my patience and wished I had some help. She told me briefly about missing her home country of Guatemala, then stepped off the train with a smile. I took a risk getting involved, but felt it was the right thing to do. As I am writing this, I have to wonder: Did she feel there was any option to tell me to mind my own business if she had wanted to? What kinds of power did she feel I had or she had?

Not long after that day, I was on the orange line subway again, this time heading home late from work. Across from me, a mom started berating and smacking her teen daughter, telling her she was stupid, a mistake, and a bitch. Both were Black. I looked around in a panic. Unlike the other train ride, this time the car was not packed, there were maybe a dozen people sitting near the duo. Most of the other passengers were Black, and dressed like me, in professional work clothes. Everyone looked uncomfortable, strained. Should I try to intervene? Was there a chance I was mis-reading the situation or that by stepping in as a white person I might make matters worse? Was it inappropriate for me to step in? I could barely stand to watch this girl shrink from the occasional slap, and from her mom's verbal onslaught. None of us did anything.

Once the mother and daughter got off, all the passengers looked around at each other and let out a collective sigh. Was I wrong to keep quiet? From what I understand about anger and abuse in families, intervening in a confrontational way in a public setting like that is really dicey, although it's awfully tempting to say, "Listen lady, you hit that kid again and I will knock you out." It might stop the violence at the moment, but most likely the parent will later take out her embarrassment on the kid. However, what does sometimes work is redirecting the aggressor into a conversation, or engaging the teen — "Hey you look familiar; where do you go to school?" or "Beautiful braids; I need a new place to take my daughter; where do you go?" That can make the adult stop and realize she is being watched, and give the teen a message that the adults around her notice and care. I just didn't know how to do it, as the sole white person on the train. But what happens to a teen like that when people watch and no one says anything? Is it even worse than what her mom is doing to her? Was I right to hold back on using the power of my voice in that instance, or was I using my whiteness as an excuse not to do anything?

Social justice isn't just about huge policy changes or widespread protests. It's a daily lived reality, the power to choose how to interact with others and how to promote our values.

Being white is part of the personal power many people have in this country. As we work for racial equity, we can also deploy that power simply by naming what is happening, as I discuss in Chapter 1. We can ask questions and encourage others to ask.

In 1982, I signed up to become a tutor in a group home, through a program called A Better Chance (ABC). It was my junior year of college. I wanted to take time off, make some money, and explore my interest in human services, to find out if that was really my calling. So off to upstate New York I went.

The ABC program brought city teenagers, ages 14–17, to a group house in suburban communities, to live, study, and prepare to make it into college. When I arrived by Greyhound bus at the large white colonial, there they were in the pristine living room: nine African American and Puerto Rican teen girls, along with the newly assigned house parents, a white, cherub-faced born-again Christian couple in their early 30s who had entered the program as their mission.

I was the live-in tutor assigned to oversee the girls' homework every evening and on Sundays — me, the white Jewish girl and budding feminist, who was trying to figure out if she was gay or straight or somewhere in between. In a town called Manlius. I dragged my suitcase upstairs and settled into the tiny bedroom, with a narrow bed and a three-drawer dresser next to a small window.

In my daily tutoring sessions with the girls (one-to-one and small group), I was supposed to be focusing on math, science, spelling, and geography. But we also talked about drugs and sex and birth control (when the house parents weren't around). We talked about feelings: What is it like being the only Black girl on the Manlius High School basketball team? What is it like going back home on vacations? The girls said they changed their language to fit back in, and some of them even stopped going home very often because it was too uncomfortable to code-switch back and forth, to be accused of being an "Oreo" — black on the outside, white on the inside. In between social studies and algebra, I asked: "What made you choose this program? What parts work for you? What about the house parents and tutors, none of us being Black or Latino — is that right?" We talked about everything.

One weekend, three of my friends from college came to visit. The girls at ABC loved hanging out with Kate, Sue, and Cady. After my friends left, I overheard two of the girls making anti-gay comments in reaction to something they saw in the newspaper, so I mentioned casually that of the three cool friends who had just visited, one was a lesbian, one was straight, and the other was bisexual. My students were shocked. They had all kinds of questions about gay people. I wanted to use my personal power to give them access to information. Hey, I suggested, why don't we write a letter to my friend who is a lesbian and ask her all your questions?

So they did, and they gathered excitedly when the answers came back in the mail. This was 1986, before most people had computer access, and before email and cellphones; letters were a big deal.

As my time tutoring in this group home came to an end, one of the kids came over to the study table in the living room and plopped down next to me. Marisol was a spunky, super-smart 10th grader from a really rough home and even rougher neighborhood in Queens. I remember the grin on her face as she took my hand, looked me in the eye, and said, "Laurie, I'll miss you. You are a really good tutor . . . but you got some crazy-ass ideas!" I smiled, wondering, but not asking, which ideas she thought were crazy: Girls can strive to be anything they want to be, Puerto Rican girls can strive to be anything they want to be, Puerto Rican girls born into poverty can strive to be anything they want to be, or something else altogether?

Another kind of power question I have wrestled with is juggling how to use my own abilities — as a writer, public speaker, and social justice advocate — and use my passion for work and activism, but still maintain my privacy and sanity, especially as a mom. And how to avoid feeling like I'm not doing enough when I observe other people putting what seems to me like all their time into social justice work.

When the mayor was running for his fourth term, in 2005, people working on his campaign asked me to get involved. It seems like a no-brainer that I would; a skeptic might argue it was primarily to keep my job (making sure he didn't get voted out) or prove my loyalty (so I didn't get booted out). But I truly wanted to, because I believed in how Tom Menino was transforming the city. And with the recession beginning, I was deeply concerned about the risk to Boston of a change in leadership.

When I thought long and hard about how to contribute, it wasn't out of ambivalence about power or about the mayor, but concern about time away from my kids, who were in elementary school and preschool at the time. I was exhausted already, between work and parenting and a bit of involvement in the kids' school. I saw other people working night and day, and I just didn't have the energy to stand on street corners, make dozens of calls, knock on hundreds of doors. I decided to pen a letter to 300 people documenting the mayor's achievements. I targeted people who were on the rolls of active voters: those who already knew and respected him (to rev them up to get out and vote), others who had come to take him for granted, who might think there was no need to vote, and people who might be ignorant of what the mayor had accomplished. I was so relieved when the mayor's top advisor told me he was pleased with the letter and had shared it with others who might draft their own version for outreach. I snail-mailed the letter out, with hand-written notes on them. That was all I felt I could do at that point with my personal power.

Back to people who are in formal positions of power: Do you think we should ever make exceptions for them, treating them as better than or different from others? I believe the exceptions should be extraordinarily rare. People in positions of power get used to being accommodated. I watched regularly in City Hall as, right next to the sign that proclaims "EVERYONE will need to go through the metal detectors," guards often waved aside city councilors, or the city councilors themselves walked right around the metal detectors, assuming they didn't need to be screened. It creeped me out. Why? In 1979, San Francisco City Councilor Dan White entered City Hall with a gun and shot to death Mayor Moscone and fellow councilor (out gay activist) Harvey Milk. I lived in San Francisco then and can still remember my high school Spanish teacher, Mrs. Trelaun, being pulled out of class, then stumbling back in to announce that our mayor had been murdered by a city councilor. While that is an extreme example, I think it's fair to assume we should hold any elected official to the same standards as the rest of us, for their sake and ours.

The bumper sticker and T-shirt slogan "Question Authority," popularized during the 1960s, has always spoken to me. It doesn't just mean to challenge or confront authority, although there are certainly times that is essential, such as when in 2004, soldiers reported on their peers and superiors at Abu Ghraib prison in Iraq who were humiliating and abusing prisoners. To me the phrase is literal: we should all feel empowered and emboldened simply to ask questions of those in power, to truly understand the thought behind rules, choices, and commands.

I value the example of people in power who have stayed grounded. Former Massachusetts Governor Michael Dukakis was famous for using the subway even while serving in the state's highest office. It wasn't a ploy to position himself as a man of the people; he truly preferred not to be chauffeured around or to waste fuel, and to have a chance to talk to the people he was representing and governing.

A book I read to my kids when they were small nails it: *Everyone Poops*. Those in positions of power do often have trouble retaining humility, accepting the reality that we all matter equally. Which means we all have a responsibility to look at what power we have and how we want to use it. The most common way people give up their power is by assuming they don't have any.

Sure, some people are a very big deal in a public way, crafting inventions, reducing hunger, creating unbelievable music that moves. And there are those who use their power in a very private way, working hard to make sure kids in their neighborhood are fed and clothed. Others make a point out of treating all with patience and kindness, knowing that burdens people carry aren't always evident.

Whether the power we have is institutional or personal, we all poop. And we all die. It is powerful to ask ourselves: In the time we have, in the ways that make most sense to us, what are the best contributions we can make with the power we possess?

CHAPTER 4
THE HUMAN CONNECTION

⚖️

*"I bring quadruple diversity to the Senate: I'm a woman;
I'll be the first Asian woman ever to be elected to the US
Senate; I am an immigrant; I am a Buddhist. When I said
this at one of my gatherings, they said, 'Yes, but are you
gay?' and I said, 'Nobody's perfect.'"*
~HAWAII SENATOR MAZIE HIRONO,
UPON HER ELECTION IN 2012

The late Senator Ted Kennedy was quite close with my boss, Mayor Tom Menino. Of the few opportunities I had to interact directly with the senator, one in particular moved me.

In 2004, at the 45th anniversary of my alma mater, the Heller Graduate School of Social Policy at Brandeis, a group of alums and faculty came together to discuss new ways to approach breaking tenacious cycles of poverty. One of the featured speakers was Senator Kennedy.

The topic of the day was asset building, a theme that questioned the longstanding notion that raising the income of poor people is the best and only approach to reducing or eliminating poverty. The researchers there pointed out that middle- and upper-class people not only have higher *incomes* than poor people, but they also begin life with (and later in life receive) assets unheard of for poor people, assets that have nothing to do with the skill or hard work of the people receiving them. These include a savings account begun by a grandparent at the child's birth; parents giving their adult children the down payment for a first home; a trust fund; a no-interest loan from a relative to start a business. Often the asset is college tuition paid by parents, allowing more economically privileged students to graduate without debt. The forum focused on new ways to think about building assets for children born into poverty. One spoke in the wheel of starting a new cycle.

After he addressed that topic, Senator Kennedy opened the floor to broader questions about national issues. Most comments from the audience were polite statements simply applauding him, missing this rare chance to tap his wisdom or touch upon controversy. I raised my hand. "How do you feel about the national movement to amend the US Constitution to ban gay marriage, and, honestly, how likely is it to happen?"

Ted Kennedy's strong reaction was noteworthy. He strode over and looked me right in the eye, raising himself up like a giant preparing for battle. He said, "Not while I have a breath left in my body will I allow the United States Constitution to be altered for the first time to *limit* rights, rather than expand them." He concluded, with certainty, "It will not happen."

I smiled, thinking about how change happens best (and is most sustainable) when it is a combination of top down (strong legislators like the man standing in front of me), bottom up (street activists drawing attention to inequity), and middle out (progressive lawyers taking a case to court, alongside brave couples going public to petition for their rights, whether it be an interracial couple winning the right to marry in 1967 or a same-sex couple in 2004).

> TED KENNEDY'S STRONG REACTION WAS NOTEWORTHY. HE STRODE OVER AND LOOKED ME RIGHT IN THE EYE, RAISING HIMSELF UP LIKE A GIANT PREPARING FOR BATTLE.

Senator Kennedy took the question personally; he viewed this attempt to change the constitution as an attack on the constitution, the country, and all citizens, not just people who are gay or bisexual and want to marry the person they love. The human connection fueled him.

For all the power of technology — including our ability to connect with people across the world in live-time — nothing replaces tried-and-true face-to-face contact. Many of us in social change movements forget this in our eagerness to speed along change through quicker means. There is no reason we can't embrace emerging communications and organizing methods, and retain the best of the old.

One of those "old" lessons learned in just about every political campaign and successful movement is this: it takes at least three interactions to get someone to consider *doing* something, *coming to* something, *becoming part of* something. I described this in Chapter 3 as a method a school employed to increase parental involvement. From getting people to register to vote, to encouraging the decision to get screened for prostate cancer or tested for HIV, to recruiting residents to attend a meeting to stop the development of a high-rise building in an overpopulated neighborhood, you gotta reach 'em at least three times, and ideally with three different methods — a mailing, a text, a phone call, an in-person visit to the home, an email, a flyer handed out at the grocery store, a photo on Instagram, a tweet.

It's especially effective if at least one of those methods is not electronic, if it includes instead handing out a flyer person-to-person or connecting voice-to-voice with a phone call. The human connection. Direct human contact. But it goes by the wayside all the time. An important meeting is announced via Twitter, Facebook, or email, with no follow-up, and the organizers wonder why only a handful of people show up.

Or we forget concerns that should be obvious, like making sure multilingual outreach takes place in the right language (or the right dialect within the language) or actually gets to the target audience. I remember a thoughtful colleague of mine at a small hospital, showing off the new brochure he translated into Spanish, looking bewildered when I asked him about the outreach plan to actually get the brochures into the hands of Spanish-speakers who might be reticent about the health care system. (We built it. Why didn't they come?) With some embarrassment, I remember having materials translated myself, only to be called out later by the target population because the translation made no sense; the "professional" doing the work wasn't from the same part of the world as the people we were trying to reach. In City Hall, in the rush to translate things in multiple languages for our work with the Boston public schools (where we had a policy of providing information in at least seven languages), sometimes it was easier to seek help from one of the dedicated staff in the mayor's office, such as the liaison to the Vietnamese community, pushing aside concerns that speaking a language is very different from being trained in translation.

In fact, I've had many of my own moments of missing the obvious opportunity for a human connection: deciding I was being too busy to send a thank you card to a colleague from another organization who helped me tour prospective funders around the city, or a condolence card to someone in City Hall whose parent died. Why would I think my time is so packed I couldn't reach out to celebrate or mourn with someone? When I receive those handwritten notes myself, after success or loss, it makes my week and strengthens that relationship. Jim Koch, the successful founder of Boston Beer Company (producers of Samuel Adams beer, among others), emphasizes the importance of personal relationships in his book *Quench Your Own Thirst: Business Lessons Learned Over a Beer or Two*. No matter how large the company grew, he made sure not to let a day go by without sending a hand-written note to an employee, understanding the importance of everyone in the company.

Maybe it was allowing my occasional shyness or conflict-avoidance to get in the way of personal contact. Yes, there were a number of memos I dropped off for the mayor that would have been more successful if I had raised the topic in a one-on-one meeting; I am, as I've said, shyer than I appear.

One time in City Hall, I avoided potential conflict by sending an email rather than walking up three flights of stairs to address a misunderstanding with a colleague. The email only furthered the misunderstanding, and that colleague then refused to accept a simple meeting with me, even though it was necessary to advance a project we both cared about. Ugh. After that, I made a commitment that whenever an email exchange has the slightest hint of tension or disagreement, my next step must be to pick up the phone or go see the person.

Other times in my career, I have revered the human connection and seen the impact. At the AIDS Action Committee, my job was to advance their prevention-education arm by training health care providers and other educators to speak about the illness, as well as training people with HIV and their family members to tell their stories, to reduce stereotypes and fear. Every speaker had to go through our four-day training, held over two weekends, and be part of monthly continuing education sessions.

I decided to run the basic training with everyone together, rather than separating out the health care professionals from the people with HIV, even though the focus of their speaking engagements would be different. These were some of the most powerful weekends of my life. This was 1989, so long ago, and yet I can still see the face and the gestures of one woman with HIV, a large, strong woman with flowing braids, a recovering addict, who spoke about her ongoing battle not to use heroin. She, a Black woman, forged a friendship in the training with a white man, both from working class backgrounds, both battling addiction and HIV. In turn, they became my friends and my mentors in courage. She went on to become one of our organization's best educators, joining the full-time staff. He — a gentle and quite funny guy, one of the most outspoken heterosexual males with HIV, having contracted it through needles — passed away not long after devoting three years to educating the public, taking a piece of many of our hearts with him.

One power of these trainings was seeing healing take place. A gay man in his late 20s, a thin, kind, hunched man, spoke of being rejected by his family once he came out to them as gay, so he had no family support when he learned he had HIV. In that same training was an elderly couple who had lost their own son to AIDS, pain etched on their faces and in their bodies. By the end of the two weekends, the three of them had committed to spending time together, the couple becoming surrogate parents to the young man.

When we honor the power of that human connection, the results are striking. Many a movement or campaign has taken off simply by putting the right people around the kitchen table or in the living room to talk to one another.

Come with me to one of these living rooms. It's a house party for an initiative called Y/BPS. I am sharing this story in detail because the lessons I learned from this initiative have continued to drive my thinking and my work for more than a decade.

But first, some background. In the early 2000s, the first decade of the century, when I worked for Mayor Menino, many families were opting out of the Boston public schools even though the district had improved more than most in the country.

Paul Grogan, the president of the Boston Foundation, invited me to a meeting with him and the foundation's education expert, Bob Wadsworth. Paul offered to fund new outreach, as one part of the foundation's strategy to keep Boston from going the route of splitting into a city of the rich and the poor, with a dwindling middle class. Paul knew that the three top reasons middle-class families cited for leaving cities were the cost of housing, concerns about safety, and perceptions about the quality of the schools. The foundation wanted to work on all of these reasons through various initiatives and partnerships, offering the mayor, represented by me that day, the chance to tackle the school perception piece by allocating more resources.

I knew that both Mayor Menino and our school superintendent, Tom Payzant, would be concerned. Would an initiative based on the idea that we need to bring other families in to the school system feel like a slap in the face to current public school families? It might come across as only being concerned about preventing "white flight" from the city. I suggested to Paul that we first use the foundation's resources to commission qualitative and quantitative research with parents to understand where their impressions about the schools came from and what made them leave. Paul and Bob agreed. This research then confirmed that most families leaving the city (or staying in the city but not using the public schools) had not visited a single school before opting out, even with all the positive changes in the schools in recent years: improved test scores, reduced teacher/student ratios, more arts programming. The thing is, we documented that this was true not just for middle-income *white* families, but also for African American, Chinese American, and Latino parents, recent immigrant families, you name it. Parents from all backgrounds with toddlers

PARENTS FROM ALL BACKGROUNDS WITH TODDLERS OR INFANTS HAD THE SAME PERCEPTION: ANY OTHER KIND OF SCHOOL WILL BE BETTER THAN THE PUBLIC SCHOOLS. BUT THEY CONCLUDED THIS WITHOUT STEPPING INSIDE THE SCHOOLS!

or infants had the same perception: any other kind of school will be better than the public schools. But they concluded this without stepping inside the schools!

Even after the research funded by the Boston Foundation, the superintendent was still concerned about this partnership with the foundation. If we developed a full parent outreach initiative, would we be directing resources — foundation, school system, and otherwise — unnecessarily toward marketing, when there is never enough funding for the work in the classrooms? Superintendent Payzant was very clear that in his experience, school systems either buckled down to do the real work of transforming teaching and learning, or they spent time and resources marketing themselves. This view, as if school improvement and marketing could not happen simultaneously, reflected the often negative perspective on marketing that I talk about in more depth in Chapter 5 — that marketing is spin, manipulative, and inaccurate; that marketing is a poor use of limited public resources, so we will get nailed for it. But I knew that Tom Payzant's concern also reflected his laser focus on improving education quality; he didn't want to take his eye off that ball. I respected that.

I was able to work with his concern by keeping the budget for this new initiative low, drawing all the initial resources from outside sources, and promising a low-key, soft sell approach to our marketing materials, not some extravagant PR campaign. This was not about billboards; it was about community organizing to talk directly with families.

I was concerned that parents would be resistant if the program was operated solely through the Boston school system, as they might feel that school representatives would be unlikely to be honest. So instead, I set up a partnership with the local YMCA branches, since the Y is a well-respected nonprofit with sites all around Boston.

The title for this initiative, Y/BPS, was a play on words: Why (Y) consider the Boston public schools (BPS) for your child's education? A team consisting of representatives from the YMCA, Bob Wadsworth from the Boston Foundation, and I designed the project. We hired parent organizers from various races, cultures, and neighborhoods, each of whom had either attended a Boston public school or had a child there, and each was based at a neighborhood Y branch to meet with families.

A key component of the work: house parties for parents of young children to learn about the schools. As word spread about the house parties, demand grew. Some people came before they even had children, while pregnant, eager to know the real deal on our city's schools, so they could plan on whether to stay or leave the city.

Now, come with me.

You are a 35-year-old, middle-income professional mother of two, a Latina mom who is a social worker, and you love living in the culturally diverse neighborhood of Jamaica Plain in Boston. You went to private school growing up, and you can't fathom sending your kids to the local public schools, especially since in Massachusetts, a program offers the option of enrolling your twin daughters in a suburban system outside the city, for free, with access to a bus that gets them to school. Your friends insisted you and your husband sign up back when you were pregnant, so, now age four, the twins are high on that wait list.

Or you are a dad from India, a physician. You believe in public schools and plan to make it work. Your wife asked you to go to a neighbor's home for a meeting to figure out how the heck to pick a public school when there are more than 10 to choose from in your neighborhood. Your kids are one and three years old.

Or you are a white woman, pregnant with your first child, doing okay financially, but struggling to pay off college loans and make the mortgage payments. Your wife just got a good job offer in another city, and she insists you ought to move, even though you both love Boston, because "the public schools here are no good anyway and we can't afford private school."

You could be any one of these parents or similar adults who came to our meetings.

You've signed up for a "Y/BPS house party" by emailing an RSVP to the name on the flyer you saw at your child's favorite playground. To last through the elements, the flyers were placed in a plastic sheet protector and taped securely to the playground fences and benches. The flyer listed six evening dates when parents could come to a house nearby to learn about the public schools. You had to send an email or text to get the location of the person's home.

You've received one text confirming the date you chose, an email a few days before the event with the agenda and encouraging words, and a phone call reminder the day before the party from a woman who herself has three kids in the school system. You aren't aware of it, but the event organizer has consciously reached out to you three times, without seeming too intrusive, to make sure you come. *Okay, okay, I'll go*, you decide, *even though none of my friends is available to join me.*

Jazz music is playing quietly as you enter a stranger's home, snacks laid out on the same table as some basic information about the school system and a name tag for you. (The host doesn't mention this, but writing out the name tags beforehand allows her quickly to figure out at the end of the meeting who didn't make it out of the 25 participants who had RSVPed, so she can follow up with them.)

The host and the evening's facilitator each welcome you warmly, as you nervously look around wondering if you will know anyone and if others will think your questions about the schools are neurotic. It's tempting to slip back out. You wonder why you bothered to come, since you'll be moving, taking the wait list spot for a suburban school, or trying to find a way to afford private tuition.

Relief sets in when you see the room fill with 20 parents as nervous as you, some of whom look familiar from the ice cream store, soccer field, subway, playground. After intros, the facilitator asks everyone to take a notecard and write down three things you remember most positively about your own education growing up. You scribble "great math teacher, music class, playing sports."

The facilitator then asks everyone to call out their questions and concerns about the schools, to make sure each topic will get addressed during the meeting. Suddenly the room falls silent. She breaks the ice with, "C'mon, we do these in people's homes so *we* can *tell* it like it is and *you* can *ask* it like it is. It's okay if your question is: 'Don't the schools really suck?!'"

Everyone laughs, and the questions are flying now: What is a charter school and how is it different from a regular school? What is the class size and teacher ratio in the Boston public schools? Are there arts and music and gym classes in the schools anymore? How do I understand and compare test scores? The questions fill two flipchart pages.

The agenda consists of 45 minutes on whether the schools are any good (what they have to offer and how they have changed in the past five years), and then another 30 minutes on how school choice works, before ending with time for people to come up individually to ask questions. Joining the facilitator are two other Boston public school parents, volunteers who are happy to answer questions about their kids' experiences.

As you realize the three of them aren't there to swindle you into sending your kid to schools in the city, but to separate myth from reality, you relax a little. It helps when the facilitator jokes that she is an education snob who went to an Ivy League school and has a master's degree, and names one of your concerns — she would never send her kids to public school just for the sake of being politically correct; she honestly loves the local school. An African American parent speaker talks about how she finds it sad that many of her neighbors who are Black or Latino automatically sign their kids up for that suburban program even when there are good public schools five blocks away that they have never visited.

Another mom raves about the diversity of the Boston schools, how her bi-cultural family feels welcome. She is Chinese, and her husband is Jewish, from Europe. Her kids are now in college, and she feels they thrived all the way through Boston schools. *Wow*, you think, *her values seem a lot like mine.*

Next the facilitator puts up posters on the living room wall with samples of the way math is taught in the public schools now — and you can't even answer some of the questions that the third and fourth graders had worked out easily on the poster paper! You learn that the current math curriculum helps kids understand how their own minds work, since there are often multiple ways to solve the same problem. The kids teach each other different methods, an approach which is connected to new statewide standards: students should be able to articulate how they solve problems, not just provide the memorized answer. This is not what you thought was going on in urban public schools.

You learn that public speaking is encouraged from day one; that kids create books starting in kindergarten; that most classrooms are set up with circular tables, not rows; that most cultural organizations in the city provide free field trips for kids in the Boston public schools to visit the Museum of Fine Art, community theaters, the Boston Ballet, Sportsmen's Tennis Club.

You are surprised that the class size in BPS is smaller than some of the surrounding suburbs. *Really?* You are more shocked, though, when the facilitator acknowledges that it is not small enough. She notes that 22 kids in a kindergarten classroom with one full-time teacher and a part-time aide is still different from having 16 kids in a private school classroom with two full-time teachers. She is clearly willing to be honest about the pros and cons of different school system choices.

She puts up a chart with different dimensions on the left — amount of enrichment courses, fees for the afterschool program, diversity of students and staff, teacher training, class size, quality of facilities — with titles across the top to compare your options: Boston public schools, charter schools (individual public schools chartered by the state and not part of the Boston school system), private schools, and suburban public schools around Boston. What you are seeing as the positives of the public schools echoes some of the positives you have started to read about on parent blogs.

The facilitator summarizes the experience: "It's not so different from choosing a house or a spouse. You can make a list of everything that matters to you, but in the end it's about chemistry — you must go see for yourself, which is why this project urges people to visit the public schools before writing them off." She provides a sheet with suggested questions and encourages you to ask these tough questions of every school you visit, whether public or private. Make no assumptions. Be informed. Be pushy. Get involved.

She gives you a list of "School Preview Time" sessions coming up for the Boston public schools, explaining that every school now offers at least three tour opportunities in November, December, and January, before registration ends in early February.

Suddenly everyone is trying to decide which schools to tour together, and the mom next to you shyly asks if you want to get your child together with hers for a playdate, since she has just moved to town.

You arrive home feeling relieved, confused (wondering if you should trust what you've heard), enthused. The next day, you receive an email from the facilitator to all the parents, saying thank you and providing links to all the websites mentioned. Two weeks later, you get in the mail a hard copy of the updated school tour schedule and a note from the facilitator. *Alright*, you decide, *I'll check out four schools and see what I think.*

In her thank you note, the facilitator mentions that three of the evening's parents have offered to host a house party themselves, inviting another 10 or 20 of their friends, and you decide to do the same, wanting to get this information to your own friends, and wanting their support.

Slowly, slowly, you realize you don't *have* to move, you don't *have* to spend thousands of dollars per year on private school tuition, you don't *have* to send your children on a 45-minute bus ride to attend school in the suburbs. Through an initiative like this, the idea of being part of a local public school becomes a possibility. A possibility built on the human connection.

More than 80 percent of parents who attended a Y/BPS house party ended up visiting schools, and many then decided to give it a go. The schools that Y/BPS staff focused most of their time on promoting — what we called the "hidden gems" of the system — increased their middle-income student population, while still welcoming students from lower-income families that chose those schools.

For many middle-income families of all races and cultures, registering for the Boston schools had been a last resort, a backup. Through Y/BPS and a series of other efforts that followed within the school system, the mindset switched: parents applied to several Boston schools, seeing private, charter, or suburban schools as the backup.

To this day, one of the highlights of my week is running into a mom, a dad, or a grandparent who attended one of those house parties as far back as a decade ago. It happens at the grocery store, the pharmacy, most often at my favorite ice cream shop. The common refrain: *My kid is now in ninth grade, and we would never have enrolled her in a Boston public school if I hadn't gone to that house party. Thank you!* In December of 2017 I received a similar email from a father who runs a home business fixing people's computer problems: "Did I ever thank you for introducing us so gently and kindly to the Boston Public Schools? Morgan and Maia are doing great, and my co-worker and I now volunteer to teach a Spanish class at the Haley [where the girls attended elementary school]."

The Y/BPS initiative focused on relationships, but we also made use of social media to get the word out, and then connected all the participating parents with listservs (popular back then) and blogs of other parents considering the public schools. Online surveys and the Boston school data systems helped us track which parents ended up using the schools and how the socioeconomic demographics changed over time. We used the best of the old organizing techniques and the best of the new.

I've seen examples of employing human connections used by religious groups. The administrative staff of a local temple was worried about decreasing membership, and understood that it was hard for people to feel known and connected within such a large congregation. The rabbi decided to set aside 90 minutes per week to make calls to anyone who had lost someone recently or had a *yartzeit*, the anniversary of the date when a loved one died. Through technology, his assistant was able to track this information about their extensive membership. When the rabbi called, he spent about 15 minutes with each person, asking to hear a story about the person who had passed away, whether it was two years ago or twenty. Often members receiving the call cried from sadness, but also from the joy of being able to tell a small tale about a beloved parent or about a child who died too young. Membership solidified and grew. Technology combined with a phone call enhanced human connections.

Sometimes the seemingly simplest, human-powered steps can move our work forward. In September of 2009, at a meeting of the Board for Thrive in 5, our citywide school readiness movement, I sat back and took in the size and mix of the group. It's one thing to appoint 26 powerful people to a board and list them in an annual report; it's another for almost every one of them to show up for quarterly meetings. To my right was a physician and senior administrator at Children's Hospital. Four over to my left sat the chair of the board for the State Department of Early Education. Next to her was the second in command in the state's health and human services office. Across from me was a VP at Wheelock College, kitty corner from one of the leading educational researchers in the country who was in the middle of writing a book about the impact of immigration policies on child health and development. Black, White, Latino, Asian.

I grabbed the Thrive in 5 assistant after the meeting to congratulate her and ask how she had gotten everyone there. She smiled, "I called them. Every single one. After sending out emails, of course. I have developed a relationship with their executive assistants," she grinned, "so they make sure to get their bosses to the meetings."

The human connection. One major lesson learned from anti-poverty initiatives is that simply providing referrals can be meaningless. Especially for people focusing on daily survival, receiving a piece of paper with the name and number of a needed service — childcare, health screening for a breast lump, food stamps — may not result in action. What works is a staff member following through. That can mean making the call with the client to access a new service, attending the appointment if the client wants support or needs a translator, or simply checking back with the client about how it went.

When I think about the reasons we in the social justice field don't remember to treasure direct human contact over technology, it's not just because it's easier to hit "reply all" or "forward" than it is to pick up the phone. More complex factors are at play. For example, life experiences can make connection a vulnerable experience. People in any minority group who speak out in order to put a face on an issue invariably pay some tolls — the loss of privacy; the pressure to seem perfect in order to combat stereotypes; being confronted by people who are biased. Racism and other forms of discrimination in this country continue to cause significant wounds, making it difficult to form relationships and alliances across our differences.

For any group that is in the minority or has been marginalized, forming relationships that break down stereotypes and barriers — in the workplace, in a political movement, in a neighborhood — requires meeting people over and over, forming some type of human connection that moves us beyond stereotypes. But I think about how hard that is, how often we live our lives segregated from those who are different, whether it's socioeconomic difference, racial and cultural difference, religious difference, language difference.

President Clinton's "Don't Ask, Don't Tell" policy, in place from 1994 to 2011, is an example. In addition to the fact that it was untenable, requiring LGBT people to act differently than their fellow soldiers (hiding the name of their beloved, for example), what disturbed me was that the whole concept became an accepted idea in parts of American society: LGBT people could live their lives as long as no one had to hear about it. But the problem is, people who change their minds about LGBT people being bad or evil or sick of-

> FOR ANY GROUP THAT IS IN THE MINORITY OR HAS BEEN MARGINALIZED, FORMING RELATIONSHIPS — IN THE WORKPLACE, IN A POLITICAL MOVEMENT, IN A NEIGHBORHOOD — REQUIRES MEETING PEOPLE OVER AND OVER, FORMING SOME TYPE OF HUMAN CONNECTION THAT MOVES US BEYOND STEREO-TYPES.

ten indicate that their opinion only alters once they get to know someone they care about who is LGBT, or once someone they already care about comes out to them. The very thing prohibited under Don't Ask, Don't Tell, the only way to improve conditions for LGBT people — putting a face to a concept — was the very thing the law prohibited.

In order to be accepted, people in a minority group can feel the need to be the perfect poster child — the non-threatening Black person, the good Asian, the "normal" Muslim, the non-effeminate gay man. The sense of living under a microscope. The exhaustion of answering the same ignorant questions over and over, even when asked with good intentions. Someone once asked me why I didn't grow up rich. "Aren't all Jews rich?" she asked. "I wish!" I responded.

Those of us in any minority group that is aiming to achieve equality and greater participation in civic life need to make a human connection with potential allies and with those in positions of power, and yet it can be so very uncomfortable. I've heard Black people comment on how bizarre it feels to be asked a question about race — "What do Blacks think about [X]" — as if they could speak for everyone else with a certain skin color.

When I was involved with a woman, I was asked quite a few times to be the poster child for a gay issue. I suppose it was a natural role, in that I enjoy public speaking, I feel strongly about equality, and I don't fit some people's stereotype of a lesbian — just as growing up, I didn't physically fit the stereotype of a Jew, being blonde.

I experienced the acute vulnerability of this "spokesperson" position during a live, televised town hall forum in 2005, right before the Massachusetts legislature was to vote on whether to amend the state constitution to ban same-sex marriage. I got a call at the mayor's office from the producer of the Channel 4 forum, which was going to be moderated by New England's beloved newscaster, Natalie Jacobson. Would I come on the show as a real, live gay person with children, a woman who was in a relationship that had lasted many years and might choose to get married? I said yes. After screening me on the phone, the producer called back to say I had so impressed her with my reasonableness on the issue that I won the honor, if you could call it that, of being 1 of 5 people in the 100-person audience who would be wearing a microphone, so I could jump into the conversation anytime I wanted, and not wait to be called on.

Well, now I really needed to figure out my key points, didn't I? As I have mentioned, three is the magic number when it comes to outreach and connections; it's also the preferred maximum number of talking points, whether we are talking to the media, fundraising, or at a job interview.

I decided my main points would be the same ones that seemed to have helped shift the mayor's thinking: First, our kids don't deserve to have the constitution changed in a way that would leave them unable to receive the legal protections of legally married parents, essentially creating a permanent class of "bastards." My second point was that marriage isn't only about obtaining *rights* but also about taking on *responsibilities*. My overall goal was, no matter how the event went, to stay calm. Turns out I was in the minority there; folks on both sides were literally screaming at each other and jumping out of their chairs!

But it's what happened before and after the debate that most affected me. On the way in to the studio, I saw the pastor who had masterminded the anti-marriage-equality movement, walking by. I went to say hello. He automatically assumed I was on his "side" and shook my hand firmly, looking me in the eye, thanking me for coming. I actually wanted the pastor to get that close to one of his "opponents" before he found out I was one of "them." And, honestly, I wanted to get close enough to him to remember that he too is human. People walking into the debate with me were surprised I talked to him.

After the debate, well, that's when it got intense. One church-going mother with elementary-school-age kids had spoken on the show about how awful marriage equality would be for parents trying to teach their kids to grow up to be good men and good women. Girls and boys couldn't grow up to be good citizens, she asserted very emotionally, if they didn't have a dad to teach them to be a man and a mom to teach them to be a woman. Her examples upset me not so much because of anything to do with LGBT rights, but because she thought our entire society had to reinforce rigid, antiquated notions of manhood — a dad had to teach his sons not to cry and how to handle tools (she really said that!) and to take care of his family, and a mom had to teach her daughters to be good caretakers and gentle people. One had to hope her poor son didn't yearn to be a ballet dancer or her daughter a mechanic.

Just like with the minister on his way into the studio, I wanted to talk to this woman up close after the show was over. She had spoken eloquently and seemed to be playing a leadership role in the effort to stop marriage equality. She was surrounded by some men from her church when I approached her. Since I too had spoken a couple times during the show, she knew I was one of "them." I said, "The thing that's on my mind is not where you and I stand on this issue, but what it would be like if our kids were in the same fourth grade classroom and really liked each other and wanted to become friends. Are our families really so different?" She was taken aback by my thought and before she could respond, one of the guys intervened. He actually said to me, "You know, ma'am, you seem like a good person and good mother. We aren't worried about people like *you*. We are worried about those other gay people."

I shed tears that night. It was discomfiting. On the subway, in the neighborhood, at work, I ran into people who had seen the show and were thrilled about the points I made and how calmly I had made them. But it just felt icky, exhausting, like I had become some sort of Stepford Wives inoffensive, robotic gay person. I called a friend to ask how he was holding up. He didn't address *any* of the issues I raised; he just pointed out that the legislature was about to vote, that our lives and the lives of our children were on display. During this moment, my friend said, we ought to hang with our own buddies and stop seeking to make connections across the aisles. He suggested that many of us give ourselves a week off from being in the public eye and having to try to change perceptions by being anything less than perfect.

The human connection. Human differences. A dynamic here is that often we see someone who is different from us, especially if they are part of a minority group, as *defined by* that difference. In early 2013, after my partner and I had split up, I met someone who was surprised to hear that my "ex" was a woman, because he knew I was dating a man. From that moment on, he saw me first and foremost as a "former lesbian," or as bisexual, rather than anything else I am — an athlete, a mother, a Jew, a writer, etc.

We all need to catch ourselves when we do this. We define the person as Haitian, or gay, or in a wheelchair, when actually, that is just one piece of a much larger whole. The man in the wheelchair may think of himself as primarily a talented college professor who happens to be in a wheelchair, or in fact he may identify as a disabled person. The woman from Haiti may think of herself primarily as a physician, who happens to be Black, or her racial and cultural identity may actually be a big part of how she sees herself. Too often a difference becomes a person's only definition in someone else's eyes, ignoring their much broader reality and also ignoring the many things a person who is seemingly

> TOO OFTEN A DIFFERENCE BECOMES A PERSON'S ONLY DEFINITION IN SOMEONE ELSE'S EYES, IGNORING THEIR MUCH BROADER REALITY AND ALSO IGNORING THE MANY THINGS A PERSON WHO IS SEEMINGLY DIFFERENT MAY HAVE IN COMMON WITH US.

different may have in common with us.

Race is still the difference in this country that seems the most load-ed, where I see the most continued unnamed ambivalence, or downright prejudice, where it's hardest to forge human connections. We'll hear, "We are as racist a country as ever." Or, "We live in a post-racial society." Which is it?

Clearly this is one of those questions where the adage is true: where you stand depends on where you sit. Of my friends and colleagues, most do fall somewhere in the middle of those two statements, and yet there is a pattern: in general, white people think we've made greater strides than Black and Latino and Asian people experience. What we're trying to do in this country — to thrive as a multi-cultural, multi-linguistic, multi-racial society — is ambitious … and crucial.

In addition to major events in our country, daily life offers oppor-tunities for those who are white to understand what people of color expe-rience. On a visit to a pharmacy in our culturally diverse Boston neigh-borhood recently, I stopped to buy makeup to blend and even out skin texture and tones. There were foundation shades for lighter-skinned folks like me and shades for people with darker skin. Makes sense. The make-up that most matched my skin tone, instead of being labeled beige, rose-beige, light tan — which is what it is, technically — what was it called? Flesh. As if there is only one color of flesh. I noticed this a decade ago, and was surprised it hadn't changed. At the beginning of President Obama's first term, when First Lady Michelle Obama wore a rose-beige dress, it was described in some news articles as her "flesh-colored" inaugural gown, the reporters apparently unaware of the irony.

The same friend I mentioned above, who counseled me to take a deep breath during the marriage debate, shared with me his dismay about how far we have yet to come on race. A middle-aged African American businessman who wears a suit to work, he still frequently gets followed by security or a small business employee when he goes into a store.

While in recent years the Black Lives Matter movement has thank-fully brought necessary attention to the complexities of racism, daily life itself reveals how far we have to go, and also how closely we who are not darker-skinned need to listen to the experiences of those who are. I am part of a multi-cultural bike-riding group that goes out for 20- to 60-mile rides weekly in the warmer months. We met for a ride on August 17, 2017, the day of an anti-racism march planned in Boston, one week after the white supremacist rally in Charlottesville, VA. At a break in the ride, we talked about our reasons for not attending the local event. Melanie, an African American woman, said she knew it was a nonviolent protest against racism, but she did not trust herself to remain nonviolent if a single person used the N-word around her. The new friend she brought to ride with us, a Latino man, said that the fresh air and invigoration of riding was what his heart needed most that day. As a social justice activist for many decades, he didn't need another public rally.

In a mid-career leadership program called LeadBoston, an African American lawyer explained to us one day how tiring it is to be the only Black person in a room at work most of the time. He knows he is as smart and as skilled as his colleagues, or more so, but he always feels this sense of needing to be the best, and it wears him down. He described how it can unnerve him to walk into a room of all white people, even though he does so constantly and with grace. Women often feel this way in a room full of men, as do any people not in the majority at a business meeting, a coalition, an event.

When the mayor put me in charge of one project that involved city-wide planning, I knew I wanted to ensure a diverse group of participants. It is common sense that if the program is supposed to serve a population that is largely black and brown, the planners should be too. And I had noticed in my work that when the room moves from being majority white to majority people of color, the meeting *participation* rate of the adults of color rises dramatically.

So we set and met a goal that at least 60 percent of the planners would be professionals of color. The attendance rate not only for the leaders of color, but for all members of the group, was the highest of any team I have been part of. And when it came time to evaluate the work, many members of color commented on how unusual it was to walk in the room and see not just one Black colleague around each table of eight, creating a sense of tokenism, but four or five per table. One member noted at the end of the planning process, "Participating in this group has restored my faith in what government can and should be."

Efforts like that are only a piece of a much larger puzzle. They don't eliminate systemic racism, and it is a luxury for white people like myself to take time to reflect on race, when people of color are living the experience. The national conversation about race ramps up when we learn about tragic events, such as the shooting of an unarmed Black teen by a white police officer, or a vigilante taking the law into his own hands when he thinks a kid of a different race wearing a hoodie shouldn't be walking home through his neighborhood.

To forge human connections necessary to move our work forward, we need to listen as humbly as we can to each other's experience. My non-Jewish friends were surprised, after 9/11 and the anti-Semitic rhetoric that flared up, that when I went to temple with my kids, I would always make sure to look for the exits and plan an escape in the case of a bombing. And there's the fear I hear in friends' voices when they plan to have "the talk" with their kids, young Black men, about how to handle being pulled over for an apparent traffic violation.

While we of all races and cultures aim to partner for social justice, daily life — from shopping for makeup to building a coalition — offers us opportunities to think about race and racism, raise such issues with others, and form a human connection across *differences* that without conscious thought and effort can too easily become *divisions*.

Our work to improve our country is enhanced by, and reliant on, human connections. Email, LinkedIn, Facebook, Twitter, Snapchat, Instagram are great forms of communicating and connecting. Yet none of us in City Hall was surprised in 2013, when the *Boston Globe* conducted a survey of residents revealing that 60 percent had personally met Mayor Menino, helping to explain his unprecedented, consistently high approval rating, which was recorded at 82% when he stepped down. Tom Menino might have had his staff use social media to get people *to* an event, but he understood the importance, throughout his career, of the in-person conversations that needed to happen *during* the event.

Even after years in the job, this mayor, known as the Urban Mechanic, never stopped holding spring conversations in a park in each neighborhood, where residents received a free plant and shared concerns about the community, or monthly evening gatherings at local diners to welcome new homeowners in each neighborhood. People remember, and build on, that personal phone call, that actual handshake, that conversation on the street. At an interfaith service that took place after the April 2013 Boston Marathon bombing, Massachusetts Governor Deval Patrick said, "We will survive and thrive because we turn TO each other, we don't turn ON each other."

When I find my work seems stuck, wondering why a team isn't functioning well enough, or a process is moving too slowly, and I'm tempted to rush ahead rather than truly stop and pay attention to the dynamics around me, often I need to kick myself with the reminder: "It's relationships, stupid."

Chapter 5
TO MARKET, TO MARKET

Your most unhappy customers
are your greatest source of learning.
–BILL GATES

When my daughter Leah was in fourth grade at a Boston public school, I bumped into a neighbor whose daughter attended private school. Chatting about how much we appreciated our kids' teachers, she commented, "I just feel bad that students in the public schools don't have what my daughter gets. The kids are studying Ancient Egypt now, so after the teacher finished the four-week curriculum, they visited the science museum and spent time with the mummies."

There wasn't an easy way for me to respond without seeming defensive, so I kept it light and simple. But here's the real deal: Leah's class had been studying Ancient Egypt too; it was part of statewide curriculum standards, not just taught in private schools. After visiting the science museum, Leah's teacher invited the students and their families to spend a Saturday gathering reeds near a river in Boston to create a replica of an Egyptian boat. After this cold and muddy adventure, the students used textbook images to guide them in creating the boat, which they then sailed on a pond a half mile from the school. So much for the wasteland of public education.

Not long after this conversation with my neighbor, I attended a hearing held by the school committee, which oversees the entire Boston school system. Parents of a popular alternative school (called a pilot school) presented their case for expansion, asking to be favored over the other, traditional public schools when it came down to budget constraints.

While I understood the inclination for each school constituency to make their case, what struck me was the ignorance about the schools overall, largely due to a lack of communication on the part of the school system. A mother beamed, "Our school is so child-focused, so innovative, they even start each day in kindergarten with circle time. It's not just the show-and-tell from back in our day. These kids are learning public speaking skills at age five!" She had no idea that *all* of the city's public school kindergartens were using that method to engage, motivate, and teach. Creative critical thinking skills and presentations are now woven throughout the Boston public school system curriculum, starting with our pre-kindergartners at ages three and four.

Without visiting any public schools prior to enrolling her child in a private school, my neighbor assumed that the local schools were uniformly weak. And the mom at the school committee, along with thousands of others, had bought into the belief that in the rare cases when innovation *does* take place in public education, it is only in some kind of alternative public school.

I was tempted to title this chapter Marketing Is Not That Four-Letter Word — Spin. The most consistent lesson I have learned in my work over the past three decades is that we make a grave mistake when we fail to market our products and services. Unfortunately, those in the nonprofit and public sectors often view marketing as:

- unnecessary (if we build it, they will automatically come);
- an inappropriate use of taxpayer or donor dollars (which should be used solely for creating the product or service — or we'll get nailed for it);
- selling out (we should never operate in the same way as the corporate sector); or
- exorbitantly expensive (so why bother).

As a result of this failure to market, some of the best programs and services go underutilized, government continues to be tagged as unable to do *anything* effectively and efficiently because good work is unseen and unknown, and agencies doing the best work with a small population don't serve the broader group in need because they don't attract capital and other resources to expand.

Marketing isn't the only way in which the public and nonprofit sectors fail to learn from our private sector peers, but I believe it is the most consistent mistake made in the helping professions and in justice work. In the case of public education, reticence to market has contributed to the cynicism and lack of respect for public schools and the resulting resistance to further investment in public schools, investments which would lead to improved schools, which would lead to a better reputation, which would lead to higher enrollment, which would … you see where I'm going.

> AS A RESULT OF THIS FAILURE TO MARKET, SOME OF THE BEST PROGRAMS AND SERVICES GO UNDERUTILIZED, GOVERNMENT CONTINUES TO BE TAGGED AS UNABLE TO DO ANYTHING EFFECTIVELY AND EFFICIENTLY … AND AGENCIES DOING THE BEST WORK WITH A SMALL POPULATION DON'T SERVE THE BROADER GROUP IN NEED BECAUSE THEY DON'T ATTRACT CAPITAL AND OTHER RESOURCES TO EXPAND.

Boston has a school choice program through which residents rank in a lottery the schools where they'd like to send their children. Parents indicate their first, second, third (and more) choices. Because some schools are better known, they are chosen more often and thus are harder to get into. To address this, Mayor Menino sponsored the initiative I wrote about in Chapter 4, Y/BPS, to promote under-chosen, lesser-known, but excellent public elementary schools, those we called "hidden gems." In the early stages of the work, we brought 12 principals together twice a year to a breakfast at a local restaurant to exchange best practices for parent outreach and marketing. We provided training on communications during those meetings.

The principals got to talk specifically about communications efforts that did and didn't work. A theme that emerged during our meetings was customer service, another area in which school staff rarely get training. One principal summed up her experience, even tying these practices to educational outcomes: "The numbers of families visiting us during school choice time went up when we realized we need to treat *anyone* who walks in our building as a customer. So if a guy from UPS drops off a package, we see him as someone who might tell others how friendly the front office staff is and how impressive he found the students' artwork on the walls. That guy lives in our neighborhood and could be a mouthpiece for us."

She noted that this work on marketing actually started to get at culture change; she noticed that when the teachers in the building were clear about what the school as a whole had to offer, and the parents started seeing the place grow in popularity, both groups began to invest more time and energy in the school. She'd never before realized that marketing was something the school should do, and she hadn't had the tools to know what good marketing looked like.

These changes, though, are not easy and can feel cumbersome, especially when administrators at individual schools need to figure out improvements on their own, in isolation. So one step we at the mayor's office took, in conjunction with the school system, was creating a toolkit for every school on how to run welcome sessions for visiting parents who were deciding what schools to put down as their choices. It may sound like a no-brainer to hold such orientations, and it is done in most private schools, but this had not been practiced systemically in the public schools.

But first, we needed to change a policy. I drafted for the mayor an executive order that offered four hours of paid time off to any city employee who wanted to visit the public schools. In turn, the superintendent of schools mandated that every school offer three different time slots for visiting each winter, with a mix of times offered, both during the school day, so people could see the school in action, and during evening or weekend hours, making it easier for many working parents to visit. Thus was born School Preview Time, which continues to this day.

Mayor Menino and School Superintendent Thomas Payzant knew schools would need more than a mandate to open their doors to visitors. They knew that once students were assigned to a school (after the lottery took place), their families needed to believe the school would work for their children, and thus actually choose to send their kids there. That toolkit we provided included sample agendas for an open house and letters in multiple languages to send home to satisfied current parents asking them to talk about their school with others. Also included was a sample script for welcome calls, so volunteers could reach out to parents who were still making their decision about whether their child would actually attend the school.

Over the course of just two years with these new policies and practices, some of those hidden gems went from 1 or 2 families calling to ask to visit, to 40–50 families visiting each month for scheduled tours!

I've been focusing here on public education's bad rap, but we could as easily talk about housing. Why should taxpayers, especially those who own their own homes, care about housing the homeless or supporting housing stability for families with very low incomes? And why should taxpayers invest in creating affordable housing if they don't understand the short- and long-term cost savings, crime reduction, and positive impact on children? If we don't tell that story, we won't build our case, and we surely won't build enough housing.

It was a source of ongoing frustration for Mayor Menino that some of government's best services and facilities remained underutilized. He knew that the same people came over and over to our network of 30-plus community centers, while many people he met on the streets had never heard of these places. Boston's community centers offer afterschool care, swim lessons, elder programming, English as a Second Language classes, computer access for those without technology at home, and teen sports leagues. All are free or very low cost. Yet some centers sat empty at times; others were bustling, but with the same people every day. Most everyone knew about the Boys and Girls Clubs and the YMCAs, but not nearly enough people knew our community centers offered very low-cost summer camp.

The staff at the central office of the network of community centers worked valiantly, sending out press releases, issuing newsletters online, really working the neighborhood newspapers and blogs. But it was an uphill battle, without enough resources allocated to marketing. I was a Boston resident, and if I hadn't worked for the mayor, I would only have heard about a couple of these two dozen centers sprinkled across the city.

We often turn to marketing after a service has been around a long time, although PR from the get-go is ideal. As we developed the Y/BPS initiative, a common pushback from parents was, "Aren't the schools really weak? Why would I even visit?" I knew about many of the successes from my own experiences as a parent and from spending time in the schools through my job. I had spent time in more than 20 schools where I would eagerly enroll my kids. But there was no readily available list of all the pluses of the public schools.

Even with a few skilled staff working on media and materials, back in the early 2000s there wasn't much to promote the general district schools, certainly not compared to charter schools, which were the new product, and so drew inherent attention, or private schools, which had reasonable marketing budgets. Our school district had a weak website, basic flyers with an overview of each school that listed confusing test scores near the top of each page but not awards received, for example, or noteworthy programs the school offered. Media stories about the schools were consistently negative.

As we were implementing that Y/BPS initiative, relying on community organizing to reach prospective Boston public school parents, those families wanted examples of how the schools had improved, proof of their merit. I found that no single document summarized the progress and the successes under the tenure of Tom Payzant, who had been changing the schools at every level over the course of a decade. I set out to create it.

I turned to Mike, my oldest brother, a marketing expert who then worked at McKinsey & Company, a management consulting firm. Working with him was easy. Getting information from the school department was difficult, and not for a lack of responsiveness. It was simply because the information wasn't in one place; no one had been collecting the good news. I got the name of a key person from each department — arts to afterschool to curriculum development to science — and asked them for their best statistics and stories. They eagerly responded.

Parents at our Y/BPS house parties snapped up the brochure, with its inviting and honest message: "A Decade of Transforming the Boston Public Schools: *Come inside. See the progress. Get involved.*" The inner flap was similarly clear that while not everything was perfect, the schools were much better than they had been, and the negative reputation was outdated. The brochure communicated that the school system welcomed the involvement of the entire community in moving forward: "As we strive to meet our goal that all staff and all schools perform at high levels, please join us in celebrating these examples of progress." The message we were trying to convey: improved and continuously improving.

We knew that simply creating the brochure would be useless if there were not a distribution mechanism, one that had a human component. In addition to offering the brochure at the house parties (where parents could read the information and ask questions), we found other venues. Children's Hospital stepped up. They reprinted the brochure with their logo on the back, distributing it directly with a note from hospital leadership to their thousands of Boston employees and patients, encouraging them to visit the public schools, providing information about School Preview Time tour schedules.

The process of creating this marketing tool was multifaceted. A top education researcher, Richard Elmore at Harvard's Graduate School of Education, provided this quote for the brochure: "From my research on school improvement around the country, I don't know another urban system that has made more progress than the Boston Public Schools, due to consistent leadership and consistent implementation of school reform. While more work remains to be done, this system has the strongest plan for continuously improving teaching and learning in every classroom at every school." This national leader called me back within days of my phone message and didn't hesitate to agree to being quoted — he just hadn't been asked before. Sometimes that's all it takes — asking. We need to ask. It helps us market.

Researching the document, I got schooled. I hadn't known that maximum class size had been reduced by 20 percent in the lower grades, or that 126 full-time arts teachers had been added in the previous 10 years, or that ours was the first urban school system in the country to connect every school to the internet. Afterschool programs had doubled; over the previous five years the improvement in SAT scores in the Boston Public Schools was six times the national average gain for math. In the previous school year, high school teams from Boston had won the state championships in hockey, basketball, and football. I didn't know we even *had* hockey teams, and I worked for the mayor!

So I now had all this important information, but would it have an impact? I went back to seek advice from the corporate sector, my brother Mike, and he wasn't very impressed. "What explains all this progress?" he asked. "What are the unifying themes? *Why* and *how* have the schools been transformed? If you don't make this cohesive, your document is just a random list of possibly accidental successes that won't be replicated or sustained."

Looking for a way to frame the brochure, I asked as many people as I could at the school department: "What explains the school system's recent explosion of success?" No one had a succinct explanation. It wasn't how people were trained to think; they knew how to do the work but not how to promote it.

Nevertheless, as I compiled the information, four reasons for success emerged, which we then placed right on the front cover of the brochure:

A DECADE OF TRANSFORMING THE BOSTON PUBLIC SCHOOLS THROUGH:
- *Challenging curriculum*, for students at all levels
- *Staff development and leadership training*, for teachers and principals
- *Stronger partnerships* with parents, universities, businesses, and cultural institutions
- *Greater variety of school choice*, including new schools, pilot schools, early childhood programs, K–8 schools, and small high schools

The brochure ended up shining a spotlight on all that Superintendent Payzant had been able to make happen during his tenure, serving as a testimonial to his legacy when he retired the following year, in 2006. The brochure captured a decade of his time leading the Boston schools, carefully putting in place what Professor Elmore had described as the essential ingredients for hastening the pace of school reform in the coming decade.

Seeing all their accomplishments in one place inspired school district leaders, spurring further marketing efforts. In the years since, the Boston school system staffers have built up the marketing and communications departments, improved the website dramatically, and they regularly collect and distribute good news about individual schools and the system as a whole. Superintendent Carol Johnson, who succeeded Tom Payzant, brilliantly opened the district-wide Office of Welcome Services at the central office, to combine marketing and direct interaction with parents. The lesson: there is no conflict between doing good work and telling the story.

I've taken to writing down whenever I see decent examples of marketing and communications in the nonprofit and public sectors. Content, of course, is of primary importance. But so are sound bites, those brief phrases or sentences that grab our attention. "Magic and Mayhem" declared a flyer at my local market. It was the name of a children's theatre group, which might have gone unnoticed but for the eye-catching group name. I wanted to know more.

Marketing doesn't require an expensive marketing campaign. It often starts simply with a commitment to communicate, making use of free or low-cost opportunities. Mayor Menino's literacy project in Boston called ReadBoston developed the tag line "Every Word Counts," as part of a much larger campaign created with largely pro bono firms. A community bank put up simple ads proclaiming, "We would tell you we're the bank of your dreams, but then everyone would know you dream about banks." Long ago, state government renamed the office of "welfare" to what it really is: transitional assistance. That re-branding is a start; now tell me what the office provides, how to access the benefits, and what the impact is on the people served and on the larger society.

Efforts to expand early childhood education in this country — discussed in more detail in Chapter 10 — still struggle with how to move the public's thinking from "babies are warm and cuddly blobs" to "what happens in the early years of a child's life affects their future and the future of our country." A team of business leaders in Massachusetts who advise the region's United Way suggested we make that connection much more directly. Call it brain building and connect it to the economy, they said, leading to a campaign called Brain Building in Progress, with images of caregivers reading and drawing with children.

A related national campaign crafted a great play on words, not long after the huge bailouts of banks, referring to our youngest citizens as "Too Small to Fail."

The connection between marketing and customer service is obvious to the private sector, but too often ignored in the social services sector. Poorly paid and often poorly trained staff might be the first ones to interact with the public, whether in person or over the phone. We can learn here from our corporate neighbors.

Coffee drinkers on a budget might have noticed a shift at Dunkin Donuts shops in 2009. The staff began to do something different when customers placed an order. Instead of just hoping to get it all right — listening to "two large coffees with cream and sugar, one medium decaf with milk, and a hot chocolate without whipped cream, please" — the staff person grabs the right size cup and writes on it: "reg w/C and S," or "decaf w/M, no S." She then hands the cups to a co-worker, who starts filling the order as her colleague rings it up. When the co-worker hands the cups to the customer, she reaffirms, "Here are your two large coffees with cream and sugar and ..." This small change both holds the staff person more accountable for getting the order correct, and sends a message to the customer that her order matters. And it makes for more interaction with the customer, which creates more customer loyalty. This is now common practice across coffee shops, but it started not that long ago.

> THE CONNECTION BETWEEN MARKETING AND CUSTOMER SERVICE IS OBVIOUS TO THE PRIVATE SECTOR, BUT TOO OFTEN IGNORED IN THE SOCIAL SERVICES SECTOR.

Customer service and accountability are linked, and the most effective corporations that interact with the public know how hard it is to do customer service well, so they provide significant training to, for example, people who staff call centers. Translating this to the schools, back when we were creating the brochure about the transformation of our schools, we talked about hanging specific signs in multiple languages outside the school system's family resource centers located in various neighborhoods, where parents go to register their children for school. The school system had struggled with customer service for years — as do all large systems, corporate or public — and we had yet to get the kind of training and measurement systems the private sector often implements. A new sample sign we discussed: "Welcome to the Boston Public Schools West Zone Family

Center. In here you will find help with [X and Y and Z]. Your wait time should be less than [time]. If the staff person does not know the answer to your question, you will receive a return call or email within 48 hours."

We created a mock-up of a sign to hang inside the center at each staff person's desk:

IN THIS CALL DID I :

- ANSWER THE PHONE WITH WARMTH AND RESPECT IN MY VOICE?

- ASK THE CALLER'S NAME AND OFFER MY FIRST NAME?

- TAKE CARE NOT TO GIVE AN ANSWER IF I AM UN-SURE OF THE INFORMATION, BUT INSTEAD CLARIFY WHEN I WOULD GET BACK TO THEM?

- ASK AT THE END IF I HAD ANSWERED THEIR QUES-TIONS COMPLETELY?

- PUT THEM ON HOLD AND SEEK MY SUPERVISOR IF THE CALLER WAS BECOMING BELLIGERENT?

- THANK THEM FOR CALLING?

At my current health center, a sign greets me each time I check in. It tells me what to *expect* and reminds the staff what to *deliver*.

So much of what I am talking about seems like common sense, doesn't it? Former governor and presidential candidate Michael Dukakis told me that as President Obama struggled for years with expanding health care coverage, his own approach as governor had been simple: never hold a press conference about health care without full-time working adults standing next to him who had no coverage. Dukakis knew that opponents would view expanding health coverage as a handout, and he wanted to make sure his initiative was understood to be health care for *working* families. That is marketing and that is making it real.

The final component of marketing to think about is *marketing yourself*. My best friend's father once gifted me a gold kernel: "You have to 'manage up,' and that includes making sure your boss knows what you do and when you do it well." *How awkward*, I thought. *My work should just speak for itself. I shouldn't have to say, "Look what I did!"* But I learned otherwise pretty early when I worked at the AIDS Action Committee (AAC) in Boston, where I was hired at age 26.

At AAC, we lived under the constant threat of the budget ax. I ran the speakers' bureau. My job was to train professionals — doctors, nurses, social workers — to provide education about preventing HIV, the virus that causes AIDS. I also trained people living with HIV — primarily gay and bisexual men, people in recovery from substance abuse, partners of people who had used IV drugs, and hemophiliacs — to tell their stories in schools, at the state house, and for the media. The goal was for the public to become less fearful of, and less discriminatory toward, people with AIDS, and for people to learn to protect their own health. I knew our speakers' bureau could be cut any time; we weren't providing the kind of direct service to sick people that drew the most funding and pulled the heartstrings. But I knew what we did was extremely important, because we were preventing more cases from occurring and we were changing public perception of the epidemic's victims and survivors.

So every few months, I made sure to walk by the office of the executive director with a letter from a teacher about how a presentation had impacted her students or a thank you note someone with AIDS had sent, saying the volunteer work had made him feel hopeful for the first time in years. I nagged and cajoled and nagged and cajoled until the director finally came to one of our weekend-long trainings for volunteer speakers, so he could experience for himself the diversity of people (races, ages, generations) in one room, working together to stem the epidemic. One man in his 60s had lost his son to AIDS, and he was damned if others weren't going to learn about safer sex. A woman had gotten herself off heroin three years before she got sick, and wanted to warn others. A nurse, originally from Denmark, wanted to be able to speak with more knowledge to his co-workers at the hospital who still misunderstood transmission, sometimes putting themselves at risk when they incorrectly disposed of used needles. My director took note.

At one point, as the federal dollars shrunk, our organization prepared to lay off a significant portion of the staff, shuttering entire programs. Mine surprisingly escaped the chopping block. I learned then that my friend's dad was right: sometimes the most important marketing targets are your own, including your boss.

Unfortunately, this is a lesson I constantly relearn, with different jobs and different bosses. I did not always handle it well with Mayor Menino. It's a tough balance to promote your work without looking, well, like a self-promoter. I feared I had offended some of my City Hall colleagues with my efforts to keep the mayor updated, at times seeming pushy or self-promoting, the way I had kept the director engaged at AIDS Action.

Self-doubt can undermine the best self-marketing plans. In 2008, Mayor Menino put me in charge of creating and managing that large team from across sectors in the city, to develop the program that would become Thrive in 5, a citywide plan for ensuring poor children did not start kindergarten already far behind their middle-class peers. I started off strong in engaging the mayor in how the work was going, then dropped the ball.

My team had finished what we called the school readiness roadmap, and we were in the process of implementing the steps in the plan. The work was taking place on multiple levels — including providing essential, sometimes life-saving services to families living in poverty (domestic violence aid, access to unemployment benefits, mental health services), so they could better stabilize the lives of their children prior to kindergarten entry. That spoke to the mayor, especially when I could introduce him to a mother whose second child was born healthier than the first, after she got treatment for addiction, or a parent from another country who had found help through us to leave an abusive husband and was now running her own small business.

But the plan also included significant work on changing public *policies* to prioritize the early childhood years and improving *systems* that were designed to support the early years. So this meant less visible and less glamorous effort: dozens of meetings to brainstorm how to increase early educators' salaries in a sustainable way; or changing practices at our health centers, so that pediatricians might detect signs of maternal depression, which has a significant impact on child development. The Thrive in 5 work was specifically designed *not* to be simply another service, project, organization, or initiative. It was to be the umbrella under which we organized all existing and new work to prevent the achievement gap, looking for holes and duplication.

However, for all the work we were doing developing the program itself, we did not devote nearly enough time to marketing this citywide umbrella. We were building it, but few people knew. This was the kind of project the media would have likely been interested in covering, but we didn't reach out because we weren't sure how to make the work sound sexy enough to cover.

I held back on putting this project in front of the mayor too often; I let myself get tired of justifying the work. Mistake. A year or two into the plan's implementation, most top colleagues in City Hall could not articulate what Thrive in 5 was and did. And since we had so many existing initiatives going on to help children and families, it was hard for people to understand how having some sort of umbrella would make a difference. I started to hear: *Isn't this new coalition "roadmap" just a drain on resources that could go right to* real *services?*

I got wind that the mayor himself just wasn't jazzed by Thrive in 5, even though, together with United Way, he had been the originator. By the time I started providing potent updates combining stats and human stories, and helped him and his cabinet chiefs understand the mix of policy and program we were undertaking, I was behind the eight ball, operating from a defensive stance. I dropped off the brief memos for the mayor, instead of the much more effective approach of sitting down with him or bringing someone to meet him who had benefited from Thrive in 5. I failed to follow my own advice to make it real by putting faces to the roadmap, forgetting about the human connection. As time went by, the city government didn't invest as much money into the work as our partners at United Way had hoped. And eventually the United Way became discouraged, and it too reduced funding for the work.

It was an uphill battle during my final year working for the mayor to bring him back around to his own initial pride and passion for taking on this 10-year school readiness roadmap. He continued to talk affectionately about the various programs within Thrive in 5 as some of his favorite work of his tenure, and he prioritized visiting those programs: Countdown to Kindergarten, Smart from the Start, the *Parenting in Action* TV show, as well as long-time programs that existed prior to Thrive, such as ReadBoston. I hadn't quite succeeded in ensuring he understood how all those programs connected and how Thrive was also changing policies and practices that changed lives. I hadn't figured out how to figuratively lock him in that silver minivan for a three-day tour the way we did with the funders from the Kellogg Foundation I talked about in Chapter 2.

Marketing is always on my mind in my current role as executive vice president at an unusual place called Thompson Island Outward Bound Education Center. We own a 204-acre island with a fascinating 180-year history as a nonprofit. The center is dedicated to providing hands-on education — science exploration combined with Outward Bound's unique methods for fostering teamwork and social and emotional resilience — for youth who have grown up in low-income families and under-resourced communities.

When I was interviewed for the job, the executive vice president position had just been created, primarily to oversee marketing and to augment the organization's resources (fundraising and earned revenue) to ensure we could serve more people. Because I had worked for the mayor and still knew very little about this island just a 20-minute ferry ride from downtown Boston, I presented the need for marketing to the hiring committee. As I explained to them, I had contacted 20 people who were key decision-makers in Boston (teachers, funders, media, corporate folks) and asked what they knew about the island. One-third knew nothing about it. One-third thought they knew what it did but got it wrong. And just one-third knew correct information about this treasure in the Boston Harbor Islands. I successfully marketed myself to the hiring committee as a knowledgeable, experienced person who could change the organization's position as a hidden gem, just as happened with many of the Boston schools.

The balance of marketing your organization and yourself is tough to find. Once I was *in* the Outward Bound job, early on, I wanted the board always to know what we were doing well. I had learned my lesson with the dwindling funds allocated to the crucial Thrive in 5 initiative. A few kind colleagues at this relatively new job let me know that it sometimes came across as my own self-promotion. Ouch. It was useful to know I had not gotten the balance right.

When it comes to social services, I've learned, we've got to be proactive in prioritizing strategic communications. No matter how urgent the need, don't bother creating a new service, project, or initiative if you don't build in from the start a plan to market it — market it to the intended clients or consumers and to the larger public, from whom you may need support and funding, and market the good work you do to the people you work for.

> IF WE DON'T TELL OUR STORY, IT WILL REMAIN UNKNOWN, OR WORSE, SOMEONE ELSE WILL TELL THE STORY AND GET IT WRONG.

If we don't tell our story, it will remain unknown, or worse, someone else will tell the story and get it wrong.

If we build it, they will come — right? Not if they've never heard of it. From my corporate colleagues, and those most successful in the nonprofit and public sectors, I have learned that promotion is not equivalent to that four-letter word, spin. Marketing's nine letters power our work.

Chapter 6
WORD FIND

⚖

If it came from a plant, eat it;
if it was made in a plant, don't.
~MICHAEL POLLAN, AUTHOR OF
THE OMNIVORE'S DILEMMA AND *FOOD RULES*

I can still feel the echo of Mayor Menino's words, spoken about a year before he died. Once a month throughout his tenure, the mayor gathered all his department heads, cabinet chiefs, and policy advisors together — 80 of us. The meeting on Friday, April 26, 2013, was particularly emotional, eleven days after the Boston Marathon bombing. Our police commissioner was still out in the field. The room was filled with many other committed and tireless professionals: the head of transportation who had a role in setting up the roadblock to make sure the suspects couldn't escape; the head of public health who had arranged mental health counseling for survivors and their families, then brought them from the hospital to the bombing site for a private service before Copley Square was re-opened to the public; many people who had worked day and night for over a week, staffing the mayor's hotline to help people find their family members who had been at the marathon. Everyone was shaken; all were exhausted.

Mayor Menino rolled into the room in his wheelchair, having checked himself out of the hospital early, once the bombing occurred. We all rose to our feet, applauding, many with tears forming. The mayor spoke about meeting with the families of the eight-year-old boy and two adults killed. He had visited some of those maimed by the two bombs set off near the finish line of the marathon. There was an audible catch in his voice at one particular moment. I'd worked with Tom Menino for 17 years, and this was the only time I'd seen him cry. He started to refer to the people in the hospitals, many of whom had lost limbs, as the "victims" he visited. Then he paused, and said softly, almost as if reflecting to himself, "They aren't victims; they are survivors."

We all know that words affect us, but too often we don't use them to our advantage — thoughtfully, intentionally. Gun violence is one issue which illustrates this.

After the Sandy Hook school massacre in 2012, many noted a somber reality: Following one failed attempt at a shoe bomb, security policy changed so that we all take off our shoes at the airport. Yet after dozens of school shootings since Columbine, there was no significant change in the regulation of guns. With names like "Shooting Star," "Desert Eagle," and even "Peacemaker," these handheld weapons of mass destruction somehow reside inside a powerful force field, deflecting our arrows. To crack the shield, we must choose — and use — our words.

In a country that embraces a lore of rugged individualism, many will reject "control." So I've seen activists and commentators shift to "gun safety" or "common sense gun measures." At a minimum, we should refer to it as "gun responsibility;" this tenet reflects a value shared by conservatives and liberals: with freedom comes responsibility.

Better is to reframe our gun violence proposals as "public safety legislation," "suicide prevention," a "public health crisis," or even a "child safety plan," given that thousands of US citizens under age 21 are injured or killed annually by guns. Those of us who seek common sense legislation need to own the narrative. It is absurd and tragic that 12,000 people in the US die annually from gun murders, and another 20,000 on average die annually by suicide with a gun.

So yes, new public safety legislation can be described as suicide prevention. What is the connection? The Harvard School of Public Health noted in 2016:

> *Every study that has examined the issue to date has found that within the US, access to firearms is associated with increased suicide risk. Guns are more lethal than other suicide means.*

They're quick. And they're irreversible. About 85 percent of attempts with a firearm are fatal: that's a much higher case fatality rate than for nearly every other method. Many of the most widely used suicide attempt methods have case fatality rates below 5 percent. Attempters who take pills or inhale car exhaust or use razors have some time to reconsider mid-attempt and summon help or be rescued. The method itself often fails, even in the absence of a rescue. Even many of those who use hanging can stop mid-attempt as about half of hanging suicides are partial-suspension, meaning the person can release the pressure if they change their mind. With a firearm, once the trigger is pulled, there's no turning back.[1]

The NRA leadership understands that words matter, so they reach out regularly to their members and the broader public with fierce, well-crafted messages, and they make sure to engage rising generations. As I mentioned in the previous chapter, many of us in the social activism field tend to categorize all marketing as "spin" (i.e., suspect), or fall victim to the notion that marketing and messaging is unnecessary, believing that good will automatically triumph. We must develop better messages and invest in spreading them.

IT IS VITAL THAT WE STATE OVER AND OVER: THE ONLY SIGNIFICANT DIFFERENCE BETWEEN SAFER COUNTRIES AND OURS IS THEY LIMIT ACCESS TO GUNS AND AMMUNITION. THIS IS A PUBLIC HEALTH CRISIS.

The question shouldn't be presented as "How do we enact more gun control?" but "How do we protect children, promote public safety, and reduce the national rate of suicide?"

Once we begin to own (or at least manage) the narrative, we can name the most salient supporting points:

- *We've seen what works in other countries to eliminate mass shootings and reduce gun deaths overall.* A truly strong country learns from others.

- *Every right spelled out in the constitution has limits and context; the second amendment is no different.* For the sake of public safety, one cannot falsely yell "FIRE" in a crowded theater. Citizens do not have the "freedom" to take out a full-page ad falsely stating that someone is a murderer. We don't call those rulings about the first amendment "speech control," just as we might stop using the term "gun control." While we permit people to drive cars, we require training, licenses, insurance, and other accountability. This isn't vehicle control; it's public safety. Public safety measures regarding guns pose no conflict with the constitution or with our overall rights.

- *We will not become a safer country until we dramatically reduce access to guns — and ammunition with which to fire those guns.* Other countries have citizens with mental health issues, violent video games, people who mean to do harm to others, and schools without security guards. It is vital that we state over and over: the only significant difference between safer countries and ours is they limit access to guns and ammunition. This is a public health crisis.

- *This fight is difficult because it is being waged by a giant the likes of the cigarette industry.* While the NRA likes to position itself as an advocate for the little guy (a hunter or a man trying to protect his family), gun access is promoted in the US by a gun industry with $13 billion of annual revenue at stake. The cigarette industry similarly successfully fought restrictions for decades, even after research proved cigarettes, designed to be addictive, were killing tens of thousands of citizens annually.

Our words matter. I am wary and weary of the headlines that play into the narrative of the NRA. Rather than the constant drumbeat of "gun control," we ought to call these measures what they are: public safety legislation.

Words we *hear* impact what we are able to see, while the words we *use* reveal what we think. How many times have you heard someone in a majority group say about a minority group (whether LGBT people, immigrants, people of a particular faith), "We need to be tolerant."? Wait. Should we *tolerate* people different from us, or should we actually *accept*, perhaps even *respect*, them?

What about tolerating or accepting someone who has a different "lifestyle"? Now that's a loaded word. A half dozen years before same-sex marriage was legalized, before the concept of marriage equality even came alive for the public, a man named Dan Conley was my neighborhood's city council representative. (He went on to become Suffolk County District Attorney.) Since several pieces of legislation and city ordinances were under consideration to support LGBT people — early efforts, like extending health benefits to same-sex partners — our neighborhood group invited Dan for a house gathering at one couple's living room, packed with 30 people.

I had a toddler at the time — my first child with my woman partner — and I knew Dan had a young kid too. At one point in the lively and mostly productive conversation, Dan explained the dilemma he faced: how to respect *all* his constituents, some of whom "just don't feel comfortable with the gay lifestyle." I couldn't let it pass. "Let me describe my family's gay lifestyle," I said, "and you tell me how it differs from yours." I walked through a typical day of little sleep, tantrums (sometimes my daughter's, sometimes my own), working long hours, then laundry, grocery-shopping, occasionally getting a sitter and heading out for — whoopee — a wild night out at the movie theater. Dan got it immediately. The audience appreciated that he realized buying into the language, using the term "gay lifestyle," was both misleading (there is no one way same-sex couples live) and divisive (the ways same-sex couples live aren't particularly different from the range of ways heterosexual couples live).

Language can limit, and language can lift.

In the 1980s, a debate about the word "queer" raged — was it an empowering term for LGBT people to reclaim, a way of expressing internalized homophobia, or none of the above? Now, decades later, that conversation continues when African Americans may call one another "nigger" or gay men may affectionately use the word "fag." Consider a bunch of feminist women in their 30s and 40s calling one another "girl" after trying to convince men for decades to call female adults "women." It is worth discussing: How different is it when a group calls itself by a term that they would find offensive from an outsider?

The first time I began to comprehend how language can empower, simply describe, or alienate was during the height of the AIDS epidemic. As the numbers of AIDS cases kept rising, the language used to refer to those contracting the disease began to evolve, away from the term AIDS *victim* to "person with AIDS." The intent was to stop focusing solely on victimhood and stop letting the illness define the whole person. Then the phrase became "person *living* with AIDS," still keeping the focus on the person and not the illness, and now switching the emphasis to the goal of survival.

The way words are used and juxtaposed can give different impressions and evoke different emotions. "A man using a wheelchair" versus a "wheelchair-bound man." The wheelchair is a tool the man uses, not an object that defines and binds him. Do you get a different impression when you hear of someone living with a disability versus someone who is disabled?

> THE WAY WORDS ARE USED AND JUXTAPOSED CAN GIVE DIFFERENT IMPRESSIONS AND EVOKE DIFFERENT EMOTIONS. "A MAN USING A WHEELCHAIR" VERSUS A "WHEELCHAIR-BOUND MAN."

"A woman with breast cancer" versus a "breast cancer victim" who might eventually, if all goes well, be a "breast cancer survivor."

The term for this re-framing and reclaiming is Person First Language. The noun, the person, comes before the illness or situation. A child with special needs versus a special-needs child. These are not minor distinctions; language impacts how we think — and what we see. I cringe when I hear a child or adult described as "she is ADHD" rather than "she has ADHD" or "she is Asperger's" rather than "she has Asperger's."

While language choices are ever-evolving, and this chart[2] is only the perspective of one organization, it helped me, as someone not living with a physical disability, to see these distinctions.

From the Texas Council for Developmental Disabilities
WHAT DO YOU CALL PEOPLE WITH DISABILITIES?

Friends, neighbors, coworkers, dad, grandma, Joe's sister, my big brother, our cousin, Mr. Schneider, George, husband, wife, colleague, employee, boss, reporter, driver, dancer, mechanic, lawyer, judge, student, educator, home owner, renter, adult, child, partner, participant, member, voter, citizen, amigo, or any other word you would use for a person.

EXAMPLES OF WHAT YOU SHOULD SAY:	EXAMPLES OF WHAT YOU SHOULD NOT SAY:
people with disabilities	the handicapped, the disabled
people without disabilities	normal, healthy, whole or typical people
person who has Down syndrome	Downs person, mongoloid, mongol
person who has (or has been diagnosed with) autism	the autistic
person with a physical disability	a cripple
person who is unable to speak, person who uses a communication device	dumb, mute
people who are blind, person who is visually impaired	the blind
person with a learning disability	learning disabled
student who receives special education services	special ed student
person who uses a wheelchair or a mobility device	confined to a wheelchair; wheelchair bound

A powerful book on this topic of being intentional in our language is *Don't Think of an Elephant: Know Your Values and Frame the Debate* by George Lakoff. Describing how the Left constantly cedes ground to the Right by way of language, Lakoff cautions that progressives are so certain of their moral high ground that they miss opportunities for establishing effective language. I see this all the time, and it worries me. In the 1980s, even as they voted against equal pay, affordable childcare, birth control access, and sex education, Republicans like Newt Gingrich described themselves as the party of "family values," successfully putting progressives on the defensive for decades. As with the NRA's work against "gun control" in service of "freedom," the Right claimed the narrative.

Look at what happened during the debates over the impeachment of President Trump in early 2020. In fact, Donald Trump taught us something I never thought would be true: if an elected leader states a lie, and especially if they repeat it over and over, and especially with social media spreading the lie, it can become perceived as fact. For him it was sometimes the size of a crowd gathered to support him (the largest ever in history!) or the rate at which immigrants commit crimes (which is in fact much lower than the rate by native-born Americans, the opposite of the lie he spread).

Here is what struck me the most during the 2020 impeachment debates: Republican leaders had no shame about using incendiary language and spinning situations to their benefit, through crafty words and arguments, regardless of the impact on our democracy. I had seen it in their successful effort to prevent President Obama from bringing Supreme Court nominee Merrick Garland to a vote; in fact, they refused even to hold hearings on his nomination. (As a reminder, Garland was unusually qualified. He served as the Chief US Circuit Judge of the Court of Appeals in D.C., graduated from Harvard Law School, served as law clerk to multiple judges, practiced in the private sector, and then worked as a federal prosecutor for the Department of Justice.) The Republican argument: President Obama should not get to nominate the person to fill the Supreme Court vacancy because that vacancy came about within the final year of Obama's term; the people should have their say in the form of choosing a new president for the coming term, who would then nominate a justice. This came from out of the blue, without any historical precedence, and of course it completely spun the situation.

Look how that 2016 argument about timing then became part of the Republican stance during the 2020 impeachment trial. They argued that removing Donald Trump in the last year of his term would mean the people would not have a voice, as the upcoming 2020 election had not taken place. So now, it would seem, if you follow the argument, no president can be impeached within the final year of his/her term. But what about the first year of the next term? Well, they could argue that the people have just spoken, and elected that person, so we can't overturn their will. Perhaps then they are arguing a president can only be impeached (if he commits grave and impeachable offenses) during years two and three of their four-year term? Look at the power of spin.

The Republicans also used incendiary phrases such as "overthrowing a duly elected President," "nullifying the votes of the election," and "robbing the people of a voice in our democracy"; they insisted that impeachment proceedings inherently did such things. No worry for them that in fact, it is Congress's role and crucial *duty* to pursue impeachment proceedings if they believe a situation warrants it. The casual, and I would say irresponsible, use of the word "overthrow" particularly struck me: it aims to incite division, and perhaps even violence, whipping up fervor among staunch Trump supporters.

During the 2016 presidential race, a new term emerged: "alt-right," short for Alternative Right. The term refers to a faction within the far right, people who use Nazi propaganda terms and even the Nazi salute at their meetings. They had called themselves, and been called, White Supremacists, an inherently confrontational term: We are white and we are supreme, superior! Then some within that group decided to try a kinder, gentler term. Nice and neutral. Alt-right. I still see various media outlets struggle not to give in to this white-washing of extremist views. In the fall of 2016, the Associated Press noted, "The so-called alt-right movement is a label currently embraced by some white supremacists and white nationalists ... It is not well known and the term may exist primarily as a public-relations device to make its supporters' actual beliefs less clear and more acceptable to a broader audience. In the past we have called such beliefs racist, neo-Nazi or white supremacist." I notice some media outlets settle on the term White Nationalists. We have to ask ourselves if this is white-washing hate and violence.

Concerned that we must call hate and violence, and even ignorance, what it is, I took to the computer in fall of 2019, when President Trump referred to the impeachment process as "a lynching." My letter to the editor was driven both by this point about the power of language, and my earlier chapter on how powerful it is to make something real, in this case lynching. I wrote:

> *The most important thing Donald Trump has done for this country is help us realize how much we have to learn. When he mocked a reporter with a disability, I realized I knew nothing about arthrogryposis. The tape of Trump bragging about grabbing women "by the pussy" illustrated the need for more measures against sexual assault. Trump calling Mexican immigrants drug dealers and rapists proved the need for education about the real lives and contributions of immigrants.*
>
> *Now the President tweets that he is being lynched, and once again we must learn.*
>
> *In the early 20th century, 4,075 Black men, women and children were lynched in the US, and that is only the number of such murders that have been documented.*
>
> *What did it mean when a man was lynched? He would be dragged from his home by figures in robes and hoods, stripped, beaten and stabbed. He would feel a noose tighten around his neck and watch with horror as they build a fire underneath him. In some cases, hooded men would cut off his genitals. He would not be able to scream as the flames burned his body, because the mob has stuffed his genitals in his mouth, a warning to others to remain compliant.*
>
> *He, a Black man, would die in agony, as dozens of white people celebrate around the fire. This is what a lynching is.*
>
> *So no, the President is not being lynched, but once again he*

has taught us something: we must never speak (or tweet) flip-
pantly about that inhumanity unleashed not so long ago upon
our fellow Americans.

Words or phrases can start out meaning one thing, then get co-opted to mean something completely different. Think of the term "fake news." The likes of *Saturday Night Live*, the *Onion*, and the *Daily Show* used that term for decades to mean intentional news parodies. Stewart referred to his fake news show. Then came the 2016 election, with a candidate who tossed out random opinions and called them facts, and cited inaccurate facts consistently, once in office. So Trump co-opted the term, calling any coverage he disagreed with by respected periodicals and journalists "fake news." I've yet to hear President Trump name actual examples of respected and award-winning news outlets that have printed fake news, as in publishing made-up or intentionally inaccurate facts. So what, then, is "fake" about the news? It has moved from a term of parody to a term of suspicion to a term lacking any true meaning, while tragically undermining the value of actual journalism.

Early childhood education advocates are becoming adept at the use of language. High quality, free preschool — along with home visits to provide information and support for struggling parents — has proven to be one of the few ways out of poverty for poor children. In 2003, the group Strategies for Children hired a firm to test public reaction to "childcare" and other terms related to the education and care of young children, hoping to build a movement for universal public preschool. Their research found very little support for publicly funded "childcare," because respondents stated that childcare is a parental duty, a private responsibility. The survey showed much higher support for publicly funded "early education," even when it was describing the same program. Publicly funded "education" was something citizens could support.

I still wrestle to remain cognizant of how other people's language affects me, and how my language affects others. In Chapter 8, you'll see I write about two young people lost to murder: Bob Curley's 10-year-old son and my colleague's 22-year old. When describing where they died, it would have been easy to use the phrase "inner city" or write that they were lost "on the streets," since both of them did die outdoors and those phrases are well known to be evocative. In fact, one of these kids was kidnapped on a tree-lined sidewalk while riding his bike in a town next to Boston, and the other was trying to break up a fight outside a neighborhood bar, so neither was actually in the "inner city." In fact, the inner city of Boston — the center of the city — is one of the most affluent areas of the country.

There is a critical need for intentional language if we are to convey crucial messages to move our work forward. During the mayor's 2009 re-election campaign, he asked me to look at the draft ads a firm had developed for him. Almost all of the ads were excellent. But I asked them to change the wording of one ad that referred to "Helping Inner City Youth." That's not how the mayor thinks and talks; that phrase unintentionally conveys a condescending attitude and separates us from them. I suggested instead, "Increasing Opportunities for Our Youth," which was a more accurate description of what we were actually doing — ensuring summer jobs, more affordable afterschool programs, sports leagues, expanded options for small high schools. And by adding the word "our," we were making a direct connection — teenagers who live in Boston are part of our Boston family.

In my current job at Outward Bound in Boston, we work with middle school students and high schoolers. The question comes up often: how best to refer to the teens in order to help donors understand the importance of investing in creating educational and nature opportunities that can close the achievement gap, but without being condescending in a way that can reinforce negative stereotypes. When I asked a focus group of the high schoolers themselves what to call them, I got a powerful response: a look of confusion. "Why all these labels?" they said. "Urban youth. Youth in need. Youth growing up in poverty. Under-served. Disadvantaged." For some, the labels felt patronizing or offensive. For others, it was simply odd to be considered anything other than a person. "What am I? Can't you just say I'm a student?" Their program manager said it well: "Why not focus on their assets?" The kids agreed: "Why would we be here if we didn't want to work hard, take advantage of opportunities, go places?" So now I tend to say we work with Boston's young people; our students are smart, ambitious, and hard-working, and facing an opportunity gap.

The concern is that if the needs of our students aren't clear, donors won't donate. So we still wrestle with our language. While I sometimes use the fact-based term "students facing economic hardship," others in my office tell me that term is weak. The school system's office of equity has settled on some terms like "supporting marginalized populations," which strikes me as, well, marginalizing. This conversation continues.

Over time, one of the questions about language that has amused me the most comes from older males in the workplace who seem befuddled by all the changes around them, when they are in the position of supervising much younger women. One man in his late 60s said to me, "Gee, what do I call females, because they always seem to get offended when I call them girls? In my day, it was a sign of respect to be protective of women."

I thought a simple, tongue-in-cheek chart would be helpful:

If you call him...	*Then call her...*
A Male	A Female
A Boy	A Girl
A Gentleman	A Lady
A Man	A Woman

Usually, then, the manager will realize that once a male reaches 18, he is referred to as a man, but people still refer to females as girls even into their 30s, 40s, 50s. What's the subtle message to young females when the college basketball teams are referred to as the *men's* team and the *ladies'* team, or the *men* players and the *girl* players? It's not that hard to get people thinking about how this impacts the female players themselves, the coach's behavior toward their players, and the people in the stands. (I realize this assumes we are using gender-based pronouns, and I applaud the current efforts to question why we put so much emphasis on gender, and what this means for people who are non-binary.)

On a more intense note about language, think "murder." That word has impact few others can match. What is your reaction when you hear the phrase "hazing death"? What about "gang rape"? Both are stomach-turning, but I would argue they don't have the potency of murder. So in the late summer of 2012, when a young college student at Florida A&M University died after a beating by his fellow band members on a bus, and the headlines constantly spoke of a "hazing" or even "hazing death," it troubled me. This young man was murdered. As part of a required ritual for new band members, he was kicked, pummeled, and stomped upon. "Hazing" implies it was, you know, kids being kids, running across campus in the snow in their underwear. No, they tortured and killed their teammate. They murdered him.

I had a similar reaction in January of 2013, when a young woman from India was assaulted on a bus by a group of men who didn't know her and, apparently for fun, attacked her and her male friend. First she was tortured and brutalized, then she was murdered. Forgive my explicitness here, but part of the torture included inserting long objects into her vagina and pushing them up until they perforated her internal organs. This was referred to as rape. For months afterward the headlines referred to the rape and to the problems of "sexual violence" in India. There was nothing sexual about what happened to that young woman. It was violence, pure and evil, the worst kind of violence imaginable — not because it involved her vagina, but because she was set upon by strangers who apparently enjoyed torture. I found it disconcerting that the headlines and subheads rarely were clear that she wasn't "just" assaulted; she died. She was murdered.

As I've been advocating, naming is important, and the decision by most media *not* to use this woman's name, perhaps out of respect for her family's privacy, also seemed to lessen the impact of what happened to her. We didn't know what she looked like, and we didn't know what she was called by those who knew and loved her. Then her family themselves asked that she be identified, so she could be honored, leading to a Facebook post seen around the world, with a candle next to the words:

**HER NAME WAS
JYOTI SINGH PANDEY**

Sometimes the problem with the words we use isn't that they are incorrect or misleading or impotent. Sometimes we use insider language that simply baffles or alienates those not in the know. If we want to introduce a new term, to further or reframe the debate, we need to define it for as long as it takes to become part of the lexicon. "Food insecurity" is an interesting new term and does have different meaning and impact than "hunger." Which do you find more evocative and accurate?

During the 2014 gubernatorial campaign in Massachusetts, both candidates developed economic and educational plans that would focus on "the Gateway Cities." Gateway to what? Were these cities that sat on the harbor and so were the gateways from the water to the land? Were they the cities surrounding Boston, so gateways to the capital?

How about the word "away"? It's often seen as neutral, as in when we "throw that away." It's simple and pleasant, antiseptic, as if there is an infinite place called away where we safely put trash. But environment advocates realized the need to use images and language to point out that there is no "away;" either items are re-used, or they pile up in landfills or in our oceans. Now we see cans marked with this reality, aiming to change our behaviors: Compost, Recycle, and Landfill.

MOST IMPORTANT FOR ADVOCATES OF SOCIAL JUSTICE: ARE WE CLAIMING AND FRAMING THE NARRATIVE, USING THE POWER OF LANGUAGE TO IMPROVE OUR WORLD?

There are multiple reasons to be intentional about the words we use and critical of the words we hear, to ask ourselves always: Are we communicating clearly? Are we painting an accurate picture? Are we ourselves buying into stereotypes? Most important for advocates of social justice: Are we claiming and framing the narrative, using the power of language to improve our world?

Chapter 7
MEDIA MATTERS

*"Too often we enjoy the comfort of opinion
without the discomfort of thought"*
~JOHN F. KENNEDY

As social justice advocates, it is critically important to evaluate what we read and hear; to create our own media, rather than waiting for others to promote us; and to make the best use of existing forms of media.

Enthusiastic and yet naïve, in 2001, I contacted Anand Vaishnav, education writer at the *Boston Globe*, after he wrote a great article on an initiative I co-created for the public school system called Countdown to Kindergarten. "I have an idea!" I told him. "Why doesn't someone write about the curriculum in the Boston public schools?" I commented on the stereotype that there's no deep thinking going on — the public schools are assumed to be old-fashioned and rote. I was inspired because my then-five-year-old had come home all excited about math. She wasn't just learning to memorize numbers and facts. Her teacher would take 10 pennies, hide some under an overturned cup, and ask the group, based on what was left, to figure out how many were hidden — and then got them to explain how they got their answers, sharing their thought process. "How cool is that as a way to teach early addition?" I said. Anand was kind but blunt with me: "Laurie, my editor will laugh me out of the room if I offer up that story idea."

While Anand rejected my idea, I had established a connection with him and knew he might be open to other ideas. For every story I have pitched to a newspaper that gets picked up, a dozen have been rejected.

The key to success is to persevere.

I kept making pitches despite the rejections. One of the times I found success was when a reporter called from our local NPR affiliate — WBUR's Sacha Pfeiffer, also of the *Boston Globe*. (Sacha later won a Pulitzer Prize for Public Service for her contribution to stories on the Catholic Church's cover-up of clergy sex abuse, featured in the movie *Spotlight*.) She called me in the mayor's office about a series on various efforts to prevent high schoolers from dropping out. Sacha wondered if I could help with

FOR EVERY STORY I HAVE PITCHED TO A NEWSPAPER THAT GETS PICKED UP, A DOZEN HAVE BEEN REJECTED. THE KEY TO SUCCESS IS TO PERSEVERE.

a story on the connection between dropout rates and children being born prematurely. I told her what I knew on the subject, which wasn't much, and strove to redirect the conversation to a more pressing issue. I asked if she wanted to hear about a particularly unusual approach to getting kids from poor and low-income families ready for school, so they would be less likely later to drop out. Somehow I avoided alienating her with my repeated follow-up calls and materials dropped off at her office; she composed a beautiful radio piece on Smart from the Start, the mayor's initiative to connect parents living in housing developments with a wide range of proven services, to break cycles of poverty and connect parents to services for themselves and their children.

I was emboldened to keep at it with Sacha because a few years earlier, after Anand had rejected my kindergarten math pitch, I had convinced a *Globe* editorial writer to pen an op-ed about the Y/BPS parent-outreach initiative. Larry Harmon had kids in the Boston public schools, so I figured he might be open to hearing some good news about the school system. I called — and called and called. He agreed to observe one of the house parties for parents deciding whether to consider visiting public schools in Boston before opting out. I knew that once we got him to the event, he would be moved — and he was. Larry wrote the editorial because of the human connection he experienced at the event and because the house party made it real for him.

Together, Smart from the Start and Y/BPS aimed to make sure all kids enter kindergarten ready for school success, and that when they do, our lower-income students would be learning alongside middle-income peers, without socioeconomic segregation. We were working with and for the rising generations, and media coverage helped us engage the public, which then helped us garner more funding. I am grateful to Anand, Sacha, and Larry.

The rapid-fire changes in media, especially the emergence of social media, have made it both easier to get the word out about our work, since we can cover it ourselves, but also harder to be heard amongst all the noise. And it's especially hard for everyone to decide what is news and what is noise.

Long before the revelation of foreign efforts to manipulate our politics through social media placement of false information, a more innocuous series illustrated the challenge of evaluating information in a so-called information age. This was the earlier days of YouTube.

In a video released in 2008, *Where the Hell Is Matt?*, an enthusiastic 20-something white guy performs a goofy jig in several countries, put to music that is haunting and joyful. His video went viral. First Matt appears alone in places ranging from Iceland to Kuwait, Spain to Zimbabwe, the US to Papua New Guinea. Then a few people join him dancing at different locales, until, by the end of the video, a groundswell of hundreds from around the world shimmy with this awkward guy in their own countries' colorful attire, evoking a sense of global unity. At this writing, that 2008 video has had over 50 million views.

But later that year, Matt strode across the stage, microphone in hand, at an Entertainment World conference, confessing that, as some people had asserted, his video was a hoax.

The twist? His video about the hoax … is a hoax! Matt Harding *did* film the dancing video around the world. He was taken aback by how many people challenged its authenticity, people skeptical that others might come together through dance. After angry emails insisting the video was fake, and labeling his video "so gay," Harding decided to "confess." He wanted to make a point.

He intentionally made the confession video absurd. Matt projected onto the screen a colorful pie chart illustrating the budget for his initial video, which included such items as "Robot Uprising Insurance," to the tune of one million dollars. Without looking closely at his chart to realize he was joking, someone indeed posted it on YouTube with the title *Harding Admits Video Was a Hoax.*[1] Soon news sources across the internet picked up on the story, and his confession became fact. Just like that.

A month later at a Macworld conference, in the third video of the series, Harding reflects on the whole experience. This goofy guy with a vision and a small budget traveled around the world and danced with lots of people, a lesson in humanity. Then he taught us another lesson: the importance of healthy skepticism, the complexity of evaluating the authenticity of "news." In this information age, it's awfully easy to be bamboozled.

I'm highlighting this story also to encourage you to check out the original 2008 video: wheretheheckismatt.com/#vids (click on "Dancing 2008"). We are indeed one people, one world, and this dance across nations continues to inspire.

Today, of course, media takes many forms. I imagine by the time this book is published, new forms of media will have emerged.

We know that we should be skeptical, yet there is still something about the written word. Whether on paper or online, for some reason it is extraordinarily difficult for us *not* to take as fact what we *read*. I have had to train myself, as I am reading a supposedly objective news piece, to think, *I am reading this publication's, this editor's, this blog's take on X. It may be true and accurate; it may not.* I then ask myself: *Is what I am reading accurate, and if so, is it* complete? *What is the source? Is there a citation for the facts?*

While I always knew intellectually that there is overt and subtle bias in much reporting, it became so much clearer when I was working for the mayor, since he was in the news constantly. The weakness I saw in stories sometimes was due to the sloppiness or inexperience of a reporter (not investigating the full range of facts), or an editor either carelessly editing out key information or presenting the story in a sensational way to draw more attention to the piece. The proliferation of unchecked and unedited blogs and websites often means stories are not fact-checked, and writers can present opinions as facts, without corroboration.

I used to keep a file of newspaper articles and internet stories that were frighteningly biased, incomplete, or inaccurate. One area of sloppiness was reporting on the Boston Public Schools. Every few years another dramatic newspaper article would come out, decrying the fact that our horrible schools were driving people from the city, stating unequivocally that the percentages of parents using the schools was tanking. In fact, according to every source I could find, the percentage of parents using the Boston Public Schools had remained fairly constant at about 75 percent for close to 100 years. I often thought we should set a strong goal to aim for in marketing the progress in our schools — to move toward a city where at least 85 percent of our families choose to send their kids to the public schools — but in order to set reasonable goals, we have to make sure we are working from accurate information in the first place.

All this said, my goal here isn't to malign the media. If we understand the strengths and limitations of the sources from which we get our news, they can be of tremendous benefit. Many journalists are skilled and ethical.

I often put "the media" in quotation marks. We should keep in mind that there has never been one form of news media. Long before the internet existed, every newspaper was different in slant, and printed news differed from radio news and television news. So lumping it all together has always been misleading. Today there are many ways to report and receive information, so it's even more inaccurate to frame all these sources as one. In hoping for improvement in the quality of news coverage, and improvement in our own ability to assess the quality of the information we are hearing, reading, and seeing, it's important not to lump all sources together.

The term that works for me is "SNAC" — Sources of News and Commentary. Every source is different, even within one medium like blogs or newspapers, and in fact a snack is how I think of what I get from each. It's one perspective, a taste, not a full meal. It is often a tasty bite, not the whole pie. The SNAC is sometimes hearty and filling, other times empty calories.

To combine my thoughts on the media and on language (as I explored in Chapter 6), I think again about the example of LGBT rights, primarily because it's an arena where choice of wording has particular impact and a bias can be obvious. It's also an area that has seen dramatic change during the 21st century. On Tuesday, October 12, 2010, a federal judge finally ruled that "Don't Ask, Don't Tell" (DADT) was unconstitutional. DADT was the nickname given to Department of Defense Directive 1304.26, passed in 1993 during President Bill Clinton's administration. For centuries, military policy barred gay people from serving in the military, with the first documented case of dismissing a gay serviceman dating back to 1778.[2] Clinton had campaigned to change that. After his election, his attempt was met with bipartisan resistance; the compromise was DADT. Someone openly gay or bisexual could not serve, but asking a service member to disclose their sexual orientation was not permitted, and if an enlistee remained closeted, they could be in the military.

> THE TERM THAT WORKS FOR ME IS "SNAC" — SOURCES OF NEWS AND COMMENTARY. EVERY SOURCE IS DIFFERENT, EVEN WITHIN ONE MEDIUM LIKE BLOGS OR NEWSPAPERS, AND IN FACT A SNACK IS HOW I THINK OF WHAT I GET FROM EACH. IT'S ONE PERSPECTIVE, A TASTE, NOT A FULL MEAL. IT IS OFTEN A TASTY BITE, NOT THE WHOLE PIE. THE SNAC IS SOMETIMES HEARTY AND FILLING, OTHER TIMES EMPTY CALORIES.

Language matters. Reporting on its appeal, some reporters said the original policy meant people could remain in the military as long as they weren't openly gay or bisexual. That sounds almost harmless. Yet another way to put it: Don't Ask, Don't Tell means people can serve in the military if they are gay or bisexual, only as long as they lie about their identity and hide their families, something not asked of their heterosexual peers. That is a different and, I would argue, a more accurate way of describing DADT.

Nonprofits, government agencies, and social justice movements struggle to obtain media coverage. The work may be important, essential even, but not necessarily stop-the-press worthy. In Chapter 5, I discussed the importance of getting the word out about various programs, such as the much-improved public school options in Boston. Effective communication includes getting the word out directly, ourselves. But it also includes getting outside coverage from the media sources with a longer reach than we might have in our organizations, agencies, and movements.

Let's assume you've sent information to a contact at a newspaper, or radio station, or news magazine that feels appropriate for a story you want to publicize. And you get a response — the writer or producer wants to interview you. Ideally, you have enough time to plan and can sum up the story you are trying to promote with no more than three points. No matter what you are asked in the interview, you have to get in those points. With practice, you can be very smooth in taking an irrelevant question, then re-directing to what you really want to talk about: *That's an important question; thank you for asking. And it reminds me of …*

Remember that town hall meeting I mentioned in Chapter 4? I went in knowing I could make no more than a couple points, if I was lucky, about why it made no sense to amend the state constitution to ban same-sex marriage. One, preventing a same-sex couple from marrying inherently means their children have fewer safeguards than other children; and two, marriage invokes not just rights but responsibilities; same-sex couples were looking to commit to responsibilities, not simply gain rights.

I notice it when people who share my views are effective in their media interviews and when people on a side I oppose demonstrate finesse, as in a January 2017 NPR interview. Senator Jeff Sessions was being interviewed by Scott Simon, who asked him first about the dismantling of the Affordable Care Act. Simon then asked if it was accurate that Republicans in Washington were expressing deep reservations about President Trump just a week into his tenure, disturbed about Trump's unprofessional penchant for tweeting. Sessions didn't even try to re-direct. He stated that he was asked onto the show to talk about health care and thought it such an important topic that he would keep the conversation to that; he would take no more questions on President Trump's credibility.

Note that above I referred to the health care system being dismantled as the Affordable Care Act. Even with Obama so popular at the time, I believed it was a mistake to call it Obamacare, to tie to one person this effort to expand coverage for those with pre-existing conditions, to allow young people to remain on their parents' insurance until age 26, and more. How telling, when people were interviewed during the 2016 presidential election, that some would insist they had great respect for the Affordable Care Act and wanted to see it remain in place, but disapproved of Obamacare, not knowing it was the exact same program.

Be prepared to tell your own story so it will get told in the first place, and so it will get told correctly. Many hyperlocal publications reprint press releases. They have limited resources, and if you can hand them a press release with clear, pertinent information, they are happy to publish that release as is.

When I think about language and the media, it discourages me how easily we allow ourselves to be swayed by a blatantly political linguistic maneuver supposedly designed to help people. In 2005, when Mitt Romney was governor of Massachusetts, he professed his commitment to addressing the academic achievement gap, naming it, accurately, as one of the major social justice issues of our time. But at the same time, our school superintendent told me he was discouraged because Romney was cutting programs proven to help lower-income kids perform better in school, like tutoring, while proposing what the governor called a bold move: Romney announced that all students who performed at a certain level on the state standardized test (called the MCAS) would receive free tuition at any state college. Guess which groups tend to perform best on standardized tests? Yup, middle- and upper-class students, whose families can more often afford test prep courses and tuition itself. I saw a few news pieces mention that irony. But what wasn't mentioned was that *tuition* at Massachusetts public colleges is deceptively low, a few thousand per year, whereas the *fees* are much higher. Romney was crafty with language: the scholarships would cover "all tuition." And no, the fees were not covered by the new proposal.

There are no easy answers for how to remain vigilant about evaluating Sources of News and Commentary. We can point out to each other deeper ways to think about what is happening in our world, and we can promote sources that provide multiple perspectives and accurate information. I have committed to spend more time reading sources from the end of the political spectrum that is foreign to me.

Discouraged about the spread of false information and the continued polarization and simplification of important national information heading into this final year of the presidential election, I have just posted this challenge on my Facebook page, a place where I intentionally keep in contact with old friends and extended family who have varied political perspectives:

> *I am asking: Could we each commit to these steps?*
> - *Focus on ideas, not on personal attacks. Do not post any meme or quote that is designed solely to mock a candidate or public official with whom we disagree, whether Nancy Pelosi or Donald Trump, former Press Secretary Sarah Sanders or relatively new representative Alexandria Ocasio-Cortez.*
> - *Before re-posting a statement, check to see if there is a citation, and if so, include it when you post, or at least check the source for your own knowledge.*
> - *Identify two news sources valued by people with whom you disagree and read/watch/listen to them at least weekly for a month.*
> - *For people in your life with whom you disagree on many political and social issues, ask them to share their views on a current issue. It could be abortion, gun violence/public safety legislation, peace efforts in the Middle East, climate change, tax policy, or immigration laws. Simply listen. See what it's like for that person to be heard and truly listen to learn, versus to refute.*
> - *Share on social media what you learned from this experiment, and if anything in your thinking has changed.*

I decided to post that message after a beloved family member shared this troubling and inaccurate meme:

"If the Dems regain power, they have promised to abolish the 1st, 2nd, 4th, 5th and 6th amendments, also the senate, the electoral college, the supreme court, borders, ICE and more. When do we get to declare them enemies of the state?"

Aiming to keep things level-headed and kind, but also address the falsehoods, I commented on his post: "Oh my. I have never heard a Democrat call for those things. This looks like the definition of false information. I am also concerned that calling one political party 'an enemy of the state' is in and of itself a threat to democracy. In a vibrant, healthy democracy, we can disagree (as I do with the policy ideas of many Republicans) without calling someone our enemy. Republicans are not my enemy. Please let's all slow down, fact-check and reflect before re-posting. That's my ten cents! Luv, Laurie."

While I find comfort in the growing efforts to bring people together to learn to listen to one another, it is important to call out the difference between opinions and facts. The current reactionary movements to undermine science, to promote inherently false information as fact, and to attack the entire industry of journalism — these steps are a true threat to democracy. Whenever someone — whether it is the president, a leader at a think tank, or a neighbor — dismisses a longtime credible source of well-researched, diligent news as promoting "fake news" it is important to ask them: "Can you provide examples of incorrect information that you are referring to?" The live-time fact-checking of on-air debates is an excellent new tool, a gift to all viewers.

Will the recent and constant changes in sources of news and commentary be beneficial or detrimental to advancing social justice? I am optimistic about this, in part due to my interaction with youth. Schoolkids, even the younger ones, have more of a voice, a platform, an outlet, an audience than ever before. They often find their voices on their own. And many adults strive to help young people become informed, critical thinkers.

My brother Jeff, the middle-school teacher, requires his students to find three examples of media outlets (print or online) covering the same story, and identify differences in the articles that might be explained by writer or editor bias. My ex, a librarian, has taught courses for high schoolers on evaluating online information; she manages to slip in, with a smile, that Wikipedia is not the be-all-and-end-all, and sometimes, just sometimes, a book can be more useful than information found online.

The efforts to ask young people to form and voice their own opinions start even younger now. Pediatricians are not only giving out books at well-child visits, but also encouraging parents to promote active thinking. One doctor I know, who is Chinese and works with many fellow immigrant families who were raised to believe children should be seen and not heard, challenges that gently with the parents of his tiny patients. He suggests that, as father and preschool-age child cuddle together to read at night, dad might say, "Before we turn the page, what do you think should happen next in the story?" or "Can you think of a different way this story might have ended?

An experience in my children's elementary school reinforced for me the richness of grades four and five as a particular moment to help young people find and raise their voice, to evaluate information, and to grow as critical thinkers.

I created a public speaking curriculum for elementary school students — Communication Skills for Social Advocacy — adapted from a course I originally taught to college students at Tufts University. My goal was to teach kids how to persuade others to care about a topic or issue of importance to them.

As the 10-, 11- and 12-year-olds learn about the basics of public speaking — eye contact, use of engaging hand gestures, managing their nervousness, taking audience questions — they research a chosen topic. They can pick any subject, serious or silly, and great conversations ensue simply from kids trying to decide what they want to speak about and what their own opinions are. My students have chosen to speak out about why we should end war, why there should be no homework, how we can care for the environment, why sour Skittles are better than bubble gum Skittles, and whether pie is better than cake. They have delivered speeches on animal safety, the quality of school lunches, and why dogs are better than cats. Showing how a fifth grader can name it and make it real, one student titled her speech "Don't Smoke a Pack of Cancer."

What became clear to me is that kids are primed to be critical thinkers, interested in talking about anything and everything we adults may take for granted or shy away from discussing. They are ready and able to evaluate sources of news and commentary. They want to discuss whether someone's pay should be based on how many years of education it took to prepare for their job (a doctor or lawyer), how important the job is to society (a teacher), how much no one else wants to do the job (someone who cleans toilets), or simply how in demand the job is. In this public speaking class, they must research, evaluate, and cite two objective sources of information on their topic, such as specific animals that are now extinct or how Skittles are made; they then have to combine it with at least one piece of personal experience — for example, an observation about how a service animal can change a person's life.

Some of the speeches among the fourth graders in the public speaking class prompt profound conversations. Years ago, one boy wrote about his father, a soldier who died in Iraq, and how upset he was that war continues around the world. Another boy, then age 10 and from a family of music aficionados, raised his hand and announced, "That reminds me of what Jimi Hendrix said: 'When the power of love overcomes the love of power, the world will know peace.'"

It won't be easy to promote true news over noise, and to do so in ways that advance social justice. My advice here is:
- Create your own media.
- Find ways to advance your own critical thinking by exposing yourself to opposing viewpoints, while you encourage critical thinking in others.
- Continually pitch your viewpoints and stories, with no more than three points, as there is value in the credibility for your cause that emerges from others covering your work.

If you are seeking coverage from mainstream print and digital media, I've found that columnists, more so than general reporters, are open to new ideas from people they don't know. I can't recall if it was a principal or a parent from the Y/PBS initiative who called *Boston Globe* columnist

Yvonne Abraham, but she truly listened and went on to write a powerful piece.[3] It was so rare then (and still is now) to obtain thorough and positive coverage of urban public schools that I want to share with you the bulk of her column:

> *Summer is over for Boston public school kids this week, and all over the city, thousands of parents are actually excited about the schools their kids are going back to.*
>
> *Not so long ago, that would have been unimaginable. With just a few exceptions, the city's schools, gutted by busing battles, funding woes, and lousy standards, were abysmal.*
>
> *But it's a surprising and too-well-kept secret that a growing number of the city's schools are inspiring cultish devotion among parents who just a few years ago might have shunned them.*
>
> *A few schools have been long-adored… But over the last five years, the batch of schools at the top of the assignment lottery charts has grown dramatically.*
>
> *"When I tell them I send my kids to Boston public schools, friends of mine are surprised," says Will Keyser, a consultant at Hill Holiday, whose son goes to the John D. Philbrick school in Roslindale. "They're spending tens of thousands of dollars to send kids to environments I can't imagine are going to produce a more informed child."*
>
> *Keyser's son, who enters the first grade on Thursday, has learned art and dance and Mandarin, surrounded by children from more than 20 countries. The parent council is fervent and diverse, the teachers enthusiastic.*
>
> *What's going on in this school and a bunch of others isn't just about money, though renovated cafeterias and nicer playgrounds certainly have helped.*
>
> *It's also about former superintendent Thomas Payzant's insistence on stricter academic standards and more accountable teachers.*
>
> *It's about middle-class parents who once gave the school system*

a wide berth trickling back, and schools finding ways to get all kinds of parents more involved.

It's about marketing. For a few years these schools were clearly improving, but nobody knew about it. Y/BPS, a four-year-old collaboration between the YMCA and the city's schools, now spreads the word in community centers, playgrounds, and living rooms...

"This is not just a pocket," says Laurie Sherman, a mayoral adviser on education and one of the creators of Y/BPS. "There is a whole movement going on here."

Lest we get carried away with shiny, start-of-the-school-year optimism here, a couple of reality checks. The love is still mostly for elementary schools, and a relatively small percentage of them. Even the happy parents admit they don't know whether they'll keep their kids in city schools when it is time for middle and high school. And often test scores don't yet mirror parents' glowing reviews.

But let's also remember how far we've come since the system's darkest days: The school year is beginning and many of the city's parents feel really good about public schools.

Talk about a fresh start.

The most important lesson for me in thinking about "the media," the various Sources of News and Commentary, is to remind ourselves and others to enjoy the SNAC — and remember it's rarely a complete meal.

Chapter 8
AMBIVALENCE

There is only one way to look at things
until someone shows us how to look at them
with different eyes.
~PABLO PICASSO

Walking to the subway one morning in 2009, earbuds in place to keep up with the news, I stopped in my tracks as the host began interviewing Bob Curley, the father of a young boy who had been kidnapped and murdered over a decade earlier. How could Curley possibly have published a book *against* the death penalty? In the late 1990s, he had been the face of the death penalty cause after his son's death, playing a pivotal role in Massachusetts nearly reinstating it. Yet in the interview, Curley explained how he came to *reject* the death penalty after confronting the fallibility of our legal system, which has put to death people later proven innocent, as well as learning about its disproportionate use against Black men and people who are poor.

Somehow Curley was able to emerge from unbearable grief, wrestle with his own ambivalence about crime and punishment, and become a spokesperson, using his personal gifts, *against* the death penalty. His journey is chronicled by journalist Brian McQuarrie in the book *The Ride*.

Not long after hearing the interview, I sat over coffee with a City Hall colleague I hadn't seen in a while. I'll call her Angelique to respect her privacy. We met to talk about a public health project, but I knew we would check in on how she was doing. Angelique's only child had been murdered two years before, and the trial was set to begin. She seemed to welcome the opportunity to talk about her son, a 22-year-old who had been a mentor to other youth. He was stabbed to death while intervening to stop a fight.

Angelique acknowledged that as a result of her pain, she began to embrace the death penalty. She said she still sits with her pastor, who understands her grief and her anger and unwillingness to forgive, as he continues to try to guide her toward a different place. She told me she wants other people to know that when one loses a child to murder, there is no peace. There is never the sense of happiness one had before; there is only getting through each day and wrestling to try to find a glimmer of meaning through work and family and faith.

Yet she too was able to admit she harbors ambivalence. "Is the death penalty ever really okay?" she wondered aloud. Would the murderer being condemned to death alleviate any of her own pain? What were the circumstances of his life that led him to carry that knife? She wasn't sure if she could follow the path of Bob Curley, but she was thinking about it.

It is easy to mistakenly dismiss ambivalence, or changing one's views, as weakness. Certainly, politicians get slammed for it. It can be seen as indecisiveness or a cold and immoral calculation — raising a moistened finger to the wind to gauge prospects for political gain. But haven't many of us changed our minds over time about a complex social or political issue? Aren't many of us living with ambivalence about how to solve the major issues of our day, whether it's the Israeli-Palestinian struggle in the Middle East, the public health crisis of gun violence, or economic inequality?

> AMBIVALENCE IS THE COEXISTENCE WITHIN US OF DIFFERING, CONTRASTING, EVEN OPPOSING REACTIONS AND BELIEFS. I HAVE SEEN THAT BEING WILLING TO BE UNRESOLVED IS OFTEN A STEP TOWARD WELL-THOUGHT-OUT DECISIONS.

There is value in outing and exploring ambivalence; in fact, it may prove one of the few ways to advance our causes. By "ambivalence," I don't mean apathy or a commitment to remaining in a place of permanent indecision as an excuse for inaction. Ambivalence is the coexistence within us of differing, contrasting, even opposing reactions and beliefs. I have seen that being willing to be unresolved is often a step toward well-thought-out decisions. Another way to think about it is that, once we do reach a conclusion, if we can have strong beliefs loosely held, we leave room for growth, as we listen to others and take in new information. This willingness to change when we are exposed to new information is one antidote to the polarization and simplification that are paralyzing our nation.

In politics, the word "polarization" means extreme grouping to one or the other side of an issue. But the word has a different and equally strong meaning outside the political realm. In physics it means restricting the vibrations of a wave, like light, to one direction. Surely we need more light in the dark places where our country is stuck. In economics, polarization describes the situation where traditional middle-class jobs — those requiring moderate level of skills, such as autoworkers' jobs — are disappearing at a much greater rate than jobs for those who are in the lower- or upper-income tiers and education levels.

Polarization requires no room for ambivalence and leaves little room for complexity. Not long before I left City Hall, I was interviewed about my take on what is needed to improve public education in Boston, an area I had been working in much of the time I served as a policy advisor for Mayor Menino. The interviewer asked for *the* solution. Is it charter schools? she asked. Or turning "failing schools" over to private companies? Is it further investment in standardized testing for accountability? I responded that to me, her question was a symptom of the problem. "The answer" lies in working on many spokes simultaneously. By seeking the one answer, we miss the other spokes on the wheel.

That spoke analogy came to me during my first 100-mile fundraiser bike ride in 2009, a journey that proved treacherous. Sweating and groaning up a hill 99 miles into our ride, my fearless biking partner, Matt LiPuma, rode over an acorn. The speed of his bike turned it into a projectile, which hit my wheel, slightly bending one of the spokes. We were determined to finish that final mile (juicy burgers and thick smoothies awaited), yet every single push of the pedals was excruciating, all because the simple machine designed to propel me forward was now the force holding me back. Changing only one spoke in the wheel threw off my whole cadence.

The irony didn't escape me that just before my spoke was damaged, Matt (who runs the Family Nurturing Center) and I had been discussing how to improve the trajectory for children born into poverty. One tiny change in the equipment I was using to get from point A to point B, and my trajectory was significantly altered.

What does it look like to push ourselves beyond polarization and oversimplification, but not to be paralyzed by complexity? In education, for example, how do we balance not rushing to judgment on education reform (insisting on finding "the solution") and yet not tolerating a slow pace of change that may leave a whole generation behind? This balance is possible; it's just not the way we are used to operating. To get there we need leaders inside and outside the education system who see the complex big picture, who are willing to rally together around a multi-pronged solution, and yet have a very clear plan to work on each of the spokes.

However, we can't let ourselves fall back on complexity as validation for permanent inaction, what some call "analysis paralysis." Effective and lasting change only happens when we can dig into the areas where we are ambivalent (often because each proposed solution has an equal down side), and when we tolerate complexity without using it as an excuse for either inaction or thoughtless reaction.

What I wish for is a combination of realism and urgency, an ability to see complexity but not be paralyzed by it. In my mind, I hold out my hands as if they are forming a bowl crafted from many interlocking sections. How can we learn to hold onto all the pieces that go into improving our country while not getting so accustomed to carrying the weight, so inured to it, that we give up on finding a solution and just drop the bowl — or become so burdened by the weight of our problems that we opt for the relief of a quick fix, sealing the cracks with soluble glue?

> HOWEVER, WE CAN'T LET OURSELVES FALL BACK ON COMPLEXITY AS VALIDATION FOR PERMANENT INACTION, WHAT SOME CALL "ANALYSIS PARALYSIS."

When those on two sides of an issue remain opponents, we fail to identify areas on which we agree and can work together. There are times when we can bridge differences and work together. For example, the Greater Boston Interfaith Coalition (GBIO) is comprised of members who may disagree about abortion and same-sex marriage, yet they have been working together since 1996 on housing, education, and health care. And the leaders of the member churches, mosques, and temples have found, along the way, that they are willing to reconsider some of the issues on which they thought they would never change their minds.

Those committed to remaining in (all too comfortable) polarized and simplified positions also miss opportunities to understand the complexity of problems, even those such as teen pregnancy, that we agree need addressing. For example, while pregnancy rates among teenage girls have gone down in many parts of the country, STD rates have not, and in some areas are skyrocketing.[1] This means that the message is getting to youth about the effectiveness of the pill in preventing pregnancy, but not about health protection, which requires the use of a condom. The danger, then, is that teens will continue to get life-threatening illnesses such as HIV, or STDs such as gonorrhea and herpes, while thinking the only issue to pay attention to is avoiding pregnancy. The health of our current teens impacts the health of the next generation to be born, and so on. If our goal is teen health, we need to dig beyond pregnancy rates, while celebrating that in some places, people on different sides of the abortion question have come together to reduce unplanned pregnancies.

Why do people tend to simplify and polarize, leaving no room for ambivalence that then turns into a new perspective? Is it innate to simplify and polarize? Some neurologists and social scientists say yes. They posit that the human brain automatically categorizes in order to comprehend, because our brain capacity is finite. Hence Blacks are X, Jews are Y, gays are Z. It need not be a minority group. Whites can be X, Christians can be Y, Italians can be Z; tall people are this, short people are that. Then when we receive new information that reinforces our belief, we take it in as affirmation; our categorizations are further strengthened. When we receive new information that *contradicts* our belief, we brand it an anomaly, an exception, which then reinforces our original belief, often our original stereotype. This process is explored throughout a fascinating book called

The Nature of Prejudice by Gordon Allport.

Others propose that evolution is a significant factor in the human tendency to polarize and simplify. The need to know who is with us and who is a potential enemy is wired into our brains, creating a predisposition against being able to see distinctions within people who are different from us; hence the phenomenon of "whites look alike" to someone who isn't white, or "Blacks look alike" to someone who isn't Black.[2] Scientists are working on ways we can train ourselves to discern facial differences in those who are different from us. Additional research, in books such as *Going to Extremes*, looks at how these possibly innate tendencies create group behavior which then reinforces our polarities.

While it gives us a great deal to work with or work against, biology is not destiny. Six approaches stand out to me that can move us away from polarization and simplification, making room for ambivalence and tolerance of complexity, which may then lead to progress on identifying common ground and seeking solutions to major social and economic issues:

1. Listen. Really.
2. Admit where we are unsure and what makes us uncomfortable.
3. Ask unexpected questions.
4. Say, "Yes, and…"
5. Respect others' ambivalence.
6. View ambivalence as part of a process, but not a place to land permanently.

1. LISTEN. REALLY.

"Most people listen with the intent to reply, not to understand." ~ Steven Covey

The phrase "We need to talk this through" tends to mean "I need to talk and have you agree." More helpful would be to remind ourselves: "I need to *listen* this through."

Winter of 2008. We were halfway through the interview with the first candidate for the director of our new Smart from the Start initiative when my colleague Heavenly Mitchell leaned forward to ask, matter-of-factly, bluntly, "Why are people poor?"

Our initiative in Boston aimed to bridge the learning gap already evident when children from low-income and poor families reach the kindergarten classroom, such as the vocabulary gap that simply widens into a full-fledged achievement gap, if not caught early. Mayor Menino felt strongly that when we launched citywide planning for Thrive in 5, the 10-year school readiness roadmap, we had to get going to support the most struggling families right away. He wanted us to look at what we already knew about improving the odds for kids, and expand those efforts immediately, while simultaneously developing the long-term plan.

Hence the creation of Smart from the Start. The program was to be launched in three Boston neighborhoods, bringing programming right to families in our housing developments, specifically those developments with a community center that offered free and available space for activities. I chose the initiative's name to indicate that children are born smart, and that we as a city and a country need to build on that inherent potential.

I assembled a cross-agency team from city government departments and community partners such as the Family Nurturing Center to identify a director to finish creating the initiative and then run it. We had narrowed the applicant pool to five candidates. The first person was a white woman in her 40s who talked the right talk but with great remove, subtle condescension in her comments about helping "those" people, bringing forth Heavenly's question. After she left, I reminded everyone about our protocol of consistency across interviews. So Heavenly sprung it on each candidate: "Why do you think people are poor?"

Next came a white man, an Asian woman, then two Black women, one in her 30s, one in her 50s. Heavenly's question proved to be a key to the perspective of each candidate. I had grown accustomed to the polarized debate on poverty: *People are poor because they don't work hard or don't care enough.* versus *People are poor because they are victims of a power structure that relies on and maintains an underclass.* These candidates gave more thoughtful, nuanced answers to Heavenly's unexpected and blunt question. I was so intrigued by their responses that I wrote them down work for word. They included the following:

"One thing I will say is that poverty, from the work I've done, what

I've seen, has an immediate and physical impact on kids. You don't see poor kids laugh as much as kids who are not poor, even when they are playing and doing the same things. So whatever the cause, we've got to find the cure. Poverty takes a toll on children beyond what we have been willing to confront as a country."

"People are poor from who they are born to and then for the lack of education that comes after. People are also often imprisoned by circumstances that are preventable, like becoming pregnant young."

"Wow, let me digest that question. I grew up poor myself. People are born into poverty and kept in poverty. Bad luck. Bad choices. Disenfranchisement, loss of hope, medical issues or substance abuse. There are a lot of reasons people get into poverty, but the main point is it's horrendously difficult to get out of poverty in this country, once in."

"It's not a disease, it's a condition. My mother, a single mom, was an exotic dancer, and my family members were all in construction. Education was the only way out for me, and it was a fluke — a client of my mom's offered me a private school scholarship. There for the grace of God went I. I have to tell you, it wasn't easy, though. I remember cheating in school because I was so tired of not succeeding. Helping people is not about running their lives, but about giving them the information to consider making better choices. I wish my mother had had more options to make different choices — for herself and for me — when she was younger."

"That's a loaded question. Nobody is born wanting to be poor and not be able to put food on the table and keep the lights on. I grew up in a disadvantaged community, but we had advantages in our family, because there were two parents and a lot of love; we just didn't have money. My parents were somehow able to see beyond their circumstances. See, the tone is set early on for kids for what to expect in life. Are your horizons limitless or limited? It all comes down to a cycle. If I as a parent myself wasn't offered limitless horizons as a child, I may unknowingly offer my own children the same lack of a horizon. Children need space to dream, and you can't dream if you don't have enough to eat. But it's the same with parents. They need to be able to meet their family's basic needs, not to have to worry about keeping their children safe and having the lights on, in order to be able to think, the way many middle-class parents think, 'I wonder if my six-month-old will go to law school?'"

We hired Cherie Craft, the one who spoke of unlimited horizons. A visionary leader, Cherie helped all of us involved in Smart from the Start to manage what the mayor identified as his ambivalence, a tension in government: How do we balance compassion and responsibility? How do we support parents, knowing that raising children is the toughest job, while having expectations that each and every parent will live up to their responsibilities if they bring a child into the world?

Cherie ran with it. She hired a small team of three, and together they knocked on the door of every parent in the housing developments where Smart from the Start first operated, listening to what those parents felt they needed, enrolling them in services proven to improve parenting ability, stabilize families, and enhance children's early brain development — parenting courses, parent-child groups, financial literacy coaching. More than half of those enrolled had never before known about or taken advantage of sliding scale afterschool programs, and most had never used the local library or community center, all free. Many of the mothers reached had been afraid to bring their children out for activities or services, due to domestic violence or violence in the neighborhood, but they were yearning, we found, to connect, to learn, to strengthen their families. Some were literally starving, and hadn't known about WIC (Women, Infants, and Children), the nutrition program for women with young kids, so Smart from the Start focused on getting them food. Out of that grew interest in classes for healthy and economical cooking, which the program launched at various community centers.

Many of the fathers said they wanted to provide for their families and be a good parent, but had been stuck in the cycles of abuse from their own childhoods. Our staff, male and female, had been there themselves and made it out of the quagmire; they gently, firmly, repeatedly reached out, meeting a future Smart from the Start member wherever he was, such as fixing a car on the street. Some people needed food to get the ball rolling in the right direction, others needed adult education and job-hunting skills, while others were ready to focus right away on their children's education.

The program demonstrated a range of successes, from a significant increase in family income and stability (many of the more isolated mothers, it turns out, had skills to run small businesses but needed to be connected to social enterprise incubators) to a decrease in the factors that prevent children from being ready for kindergarten (maternal depression, little access to books, and isolation from social interactions with other children).

One of the goals of Smart from the Start was to reduce the need for expensive public school special education services, and do right by kids, by remediating problems that could have been detected and addressed early on, from autism and asthma to speech delays. The program also found that working with parents to engage their young children led to changes in the older children in the household. The staff identified teenagers who had never been to the nearby community center, connecting them to free sports leagues, low-cost summer camp, or summer jobs.

It required listening, and doing so to learn. Once the mayor met some of the Smart from the Start families, he told me it became one of his favorite programs of his 20 years in office. Respectful support and listening-led intervention helped break the patterns of polarization, the idea that nothing can be done to change cycles of poverty, so why bother.

Truly listening doesn't mean accepting; sometimes one then goes on to challenge another person's ambivalence. After hearing a family member say many times that they didn't support affirmative action because it demeans people of color who may question their self-worth (did they only get in to that college or get that job because of affirmative action?), I noted that the first and biggest form of affirmative action I'm aware of is legacy — for well-off white males. No one seems to be worried about the impact on their self-esteem when a young man gets admitted to an Ivy League school largely because his father and grandfather went there. No one seems worried about the self-esteem of a white male college graduate from an upper-class family when he gets his first job interview due to a few calls made to the firm's CEO testifying to the young man's talents. So why that particular worry about other forms of affirmative action? Sometimes

I have found power in truly listening, and sometimes following up with an unexpected question.

2. ADMIT WHERE WE ARE UNSURE AND WHAT MAKES US UNCOMFORTABLE.

Just twice, during the 17 years I worked with him, did Mayor Menino talk openly with me about areas of personal ambivalence. The first time, as I discussed in Chapter 3, it was about same-sex marriage. The mayor's journey on marriage equality started with acknowledging what made him uncomfortable and unsure.

The second time the Mayor discussed an area of deep personal ambivalence with me was during a poignant conversation about education and poverty in the fall of 2006.

While I saw Mayor Menino in City Hall or out at events almost daily, I was careful not to wear out my welcome; I picked my battles. Only a few times a year did I formally get on his schedule to present new ideas. This time I wanted to talk about our work to close the achievement gap between Black and Latino students in Boston and their white and Asian counterparts. The mayor had assigned me to a cross-department team to continue to flesh out the city's and school department's work in the years from kindergarten through high school.

I told the mayor how it concerned me that so many kids start out struggling *before* they even get to kindergarten. Given what we now know from the science and economics of early childhood, why aren't we trying to *prevent* problems that become more expensive and more difficult to fix later on? The mayor's response made sense: If government gets into the business of trying to fix conditions for little kids before they enter the public sphere of school, we will be accused of intrusion into people's private lives. He expressed sadness that "government can't give every kid what they need: a set of healthy, loving parents." He went on to say that so much of what families are dealing with is about poverty and racism, which we don't know how to eliminate. Those aren't things we want to send the message that government can be held responsible for.

"Ah," I prodded, my heart beating faster. "Sir, are you saying that while we wait to eliminate racism and poverty, there is nothing we can do for the youngest kids, even if we know that might be the only way to really solve the achievement gap?" The mayor shot back a challenge. He announced that I was now in charge of developing a plan to *prevent* the achievement gap! I snuck in one last question, somewhere between confidence and fear: "Can I use your name to raise money to create a planning process for this project?" Sure, he replied, then firmly kicked me out of his office, moving on to the next staff member waiting to talk with him.

The time was right in Boston — 2006. Early childhood education advocacy organizations had been wanting to wage a citywide campaign, starting with a citywide planning process, to look at the needs of our youngest kids and their families. A few of these leaders had been talking about approaching local foundations for support. I contacted them, and we agreed to join our community and government forces, after some very rocky initial conversations during which a gifted facilitator from United Way pushed the advocates past their skepticism of us City Hallers.

A fascinating 24 months followed. With the help of an executive on loan from Children's Hospital to staff this project, we researched the current state of children and families in Boston, mapping where families with the youngest children lived and where the population of families was growing, as well as mapping the services nearby, from childcare to playgrounds, swimming pools to health centers.

Simultaneously, we established a team of 12 top researchers and social service providers, to create a white paper on what was already known about setting young children up for success. It was led by the head of early childhood at the public schools and a researcher at Harvard Graduate School of Education. The goal was to guide the mayor on current scientific and economic information about the earliest years of life, including what interventions work with the most struggling families, with the greatest return on investment.

This work took place in the context of the lively national dialogue about the racial academic achievement gap and how to close it. This meant there was an opportunity for Boston to be a leader in focusing on *preventing* the gap from opening before kids even arrived at school.

There were many areas of ambivalence to get past along the way. For example, the team of 12 researchers disagreed among themselves whether it was more effective to focus on the earliest years of a child's life (pre-natal through age two) or on the preschool years (ages three through five). The earliest years are significant in many ways, and during that time period, it is easier to engage parents, because they show up in person to pick up a child from Head Start or childcare and take their children to doctor's appointments. That was the argument for devoting limited financial resources to initiatives aimed at families with kids ages zero through three. Yet, others argued, it is tremendously difficult to change parent and home behavior and much easier to make improvements in preschools serving poor kids who are ages three through five. Yes, but when changes *can* happen in the home and family, came the retort, research shows the impact is stronger and longer-lasting than changes suggested in preschools. Why do we have to choose? some argued. Because funding is limited, others responded; it's better to invest more in one aspect than less in both.

This work — the most challenging of my career — was worth it. In March of 2008, we unveiled our school readiness citywide initiative called Thrive in 5. Local foundations made investments, the largest from the Barr Foundation, and nationally, the Kellogg Foundation invested $1.5 million early on, followed by another large commitment. The plan has guided change throughout Boston, improving life for young children and their families in the city. Health providers began to systematically screen families for both child development concerns and parental issues such as maternal depression, that impact the growth of the child's brain and immune system. Early education quality improved, both in licensed programs and among neighbors who take in kids to their informal childcare, as systems were set up to connect with those care providers. Parents in numerous neighborhoods began training other parents about child development. In some communities, bodegas, barbershops, pharmacies, and other small businesses — wherever kids and parents go in their daily lives — took on promoting parenting skills and early reading. Thrive in 5 was eventually incorporated into a broader network called the Boston Opportunity Agenda, which tracks metrics for children from birth through higher education, reporting out annually on what they call the cradle-to-career education pipeline.

The mayor's willingness to share with me his ambivalence about the role of city government led to the creation of this work.

3. ASK UNEXPECTED QUESTIONS.

"Why do you think people are poor?" unexpectedly became a key topic in our hiring process for Smart from the Start. It got right to the heart of the fact that in this country there is great ambivalence about social safety net programs — are they a hand up or a handout? Unexpected and uncommon questions can lead to deeper, more fruitful discussions.

"WHY DO YOU THINK PEOPLE ARE POOR?" UNEXPECTEDLY BECAME A KEY TOPIC IN OUR HIRING PROCESS FOR SMART FROM THE START. IT GOT RIGHT TO THE HEART OF THE FACT THAT IN THIS COUNTRY THERE IS GREAT AMBIVALENCE ABOUT SOCIAL SAFETY NET PROGRAMS — ARE THEY A HAND UP OR A HANDOUT?

Long before he became city council president, a man named Bill Linehan was a policy advisor alongside me in the mayor's office. He once told me he wished the US would consider alternatives to our troubled transportation infrastructure. One day he leaned over into my cubicle and asked, "Why isn't the subway free?" Bill thought that while we would initially sacrifice the revenue from fares, we not only would dramatically cut the cost of operating the system (eliminating the machines and materials involved in collecting fares, and the cost of employees currently tracking fare evaders), we might change our economy in important ways. If lower-income people could more easily and affordably get to work, they might return much more to the public coffers in taxes than we would lose in fares. He wasn't sure this was the answer, but his concern was that we couldn't even have those kinds of conversations in a country where the knee-jerk reaction is that such an approach would be a handout. Bill raised that with me 20 years ago and only now do I hear regular conversation in the US about making public transit free.

The role of government and the role and scope of taxes are certainly sources of ambivalence, even among those with strong opinions. Sometimes this can lead to new approaches. In 2002, a group in Massachusetts called Citizens for Limited Taxation successfully filed a bill to allow an option for people who wanted to pay a higher tax rate of 5.85%, openly noting this as a poke at liberals who didn't want to reduce the state income tax to 5% for fear of service cuts. The group never expected anyone to pay the extra .85 percent, surprised when the checkoff initially raised $2.4 million. A decade after the checkoff option, *Boston Globe* columnist Farah Stockman questioned if there would be less divisiveness in the country over taxation if citizens could direct some portion of their taxes to specific parts of government: paying down the national debt, social programs, road repair, public education, foreign aid, or the military. Why not at least explore the question?

4. SAY, "YES, AND..."

In improv theatre, "Yes, and…" is a key concept. You never negate what a fellow actor proposes. If they say, "This bus is taking forever to come," don't respond, "No, I've only been waiting one minute, and it comes all the time." Rather, you build on that, saying something like, "I know! I've been waiting since 1965!"

I am heartened by examples of people being willing to stand up for "Yes, and…" even in times of tragedy, when the tendency might be to quash dissension or force people to pick sides.

On April 15, 2013, near the finish line at the Boston Marathon, a pair of brothers planted and detonated homemade bombs. People came together from all sectors of life and all parts of the city, state, country, and globe to show their support for the survivors and pay their respects to the dead.

Throughout the tragedy, I saw conscious efforts to frame the conversation and express the pain in an appropriately complex way, from social media to print media, radio programs to conversations on the subway, national coverage to local blogs. The older brother was killed not long after the bombing in a shootout, and the captured younger bomber lay in the hospital. Although fearful they might be seen as excusing the surviving bomber, some people posted and tweeted that they couldn't forget he was a young man, once someone's baby; they did not want to see him as inhuman, although his acts were. And shouldn't everyone benefit from the assumption of innocence until proven guilty? It took guts for them to speak out.

Right after the bombers were identified as followers of Islam, people of all religions made efforts to distinguish between Islam and terrorism, with postings on Facebook such as "Terrorists are no more a reflection of Islamic belief than the Ku Klux Klan is an example of Christianity." Massachusetts Governor Deval Patrick and Boston Mayor Menino immediately organized an interfaith service, attended by President Obama.

City and state officials and local media made an intentional effort to focus on the survivors rather than the perpetrators, with stories about citizen heroes who saved the lives of marathon watchers, and health care providers who performed miracles to save the leg of a survivor who had already lost one in the explosions. Print media like the *Boston Globe* splashed photos everywhere of the heroes, publishing analyses about how our emergency response system had fortunately been strengthened in Boston over the previous 10 years. Not a single person who left the bomb site alive, they reported, died in the ambulances or in the hospital.

Why did these efforts to manage the message and prevent polarization matter? Muslims interviewed in Boston reported significantly less fallout and backlash than they feared.[3] The focus wasn't on the background of the criminals (which often leads to casting a pall over all people of that culture or background, if the perpetrator is a person of color or an immigrant), but on the value of the survivors. I saw many examples of healthy restraint and openness to complexity, which is not common in times of crisis.

Then came the term "Boston Strong," which concerned me. In the bombing, three people died immediately, a young police officer was murdered by the brothers as they fled a few days later, 17 people lost one or more limbs, a total of 264 people were injured, and many people throughout the country felt the reverberations of the bombs in a new awareness that 9/11 would not be the only time terrorists would strike in America. While acts of terrorism happen on a much larger scale daily in other parts of the world, this was no small incident in immediate impact and in the shadow it cast.

So in that act of violence at the world's best-known road race (an event in which millions of dollars annually are raised for charity), one way many people in and around Boston dealt with their fear, pain, loss, and anger was to pump up Boston as the best place in the world. Hence "Boston Strong."

That phrase captured a need to see our home as a place of survival, as not just a good place, but the best place. While I understood the right of people to grieve as they need to, it didn't sit right with me. I was relieved when posts on Facebook and Twitter took care to remind others that some of the language used — about how this act didn't belong in Boston —inadvertently implied that it was okay to happen elsewhere in the world. That comment struck me as particularly important when exactly two weeks after the explosions in Boston, NPR reported a suicide bomber in Pakistan had just killed 8 people and wounded 80 — lives just as important as ours here. "Boston Strong, A World Connected" is what I wanted to see. Yes, we Bostonians could be amazing without claiming superiority over others.

5. RESPECT OTHERS' AMBIVALENCE.

The best of leaders grapple often with their own ambivalence about how to approach complex problems — the need to break a problem into parts in order to make progress, but without ignoring complexities that will need attention next.

Mayor Menino was very concerned about the continued poor reputation of the Boston public schools, even in the face of significant academic progress. Knowing this, even before creating the Y/BPS initiative I've told you about, I spoke a handful of times with School Superintendent Tom Payzant to understand his thinking about expanding resources for marketing and communications. He responded with two concerns. He said that in his experience, school systems that focus on marketing often aren't the real deal; they talk a good game and position themselves beautifully in the press as making significant progress, but the actual work in the classrooms doesn't hold up. It struck me that in his mind the equation was marketing = spin; he believed that one had to choose between communications and doing real work. That was one part of Payzant's ambivalence.

I knew a school system like Boston, on the right track and making deep progress, could spread the word well, without threatening progress or quality. When we did begin to tell our story and receive attention, not only did it impact parent choices, but also brought in resources: the Broad Foundation — a large, national foundation that promotes entrepreneurship in education, science and the arts — awarded Boston the most-improved urban school system in the country. This garnered Boston ongoing attention and a $1M prize to be used toward further school system progress.

Dr. Payzant's second concern was that too much work needed to be done on teaching and learning inside the classroom to allocate time and attention to marketing; there just wasn't time for both. I could tell these components that seemed so interconnected for me were existing in silos for him. Knowing that the core of teaching and learning was his passion

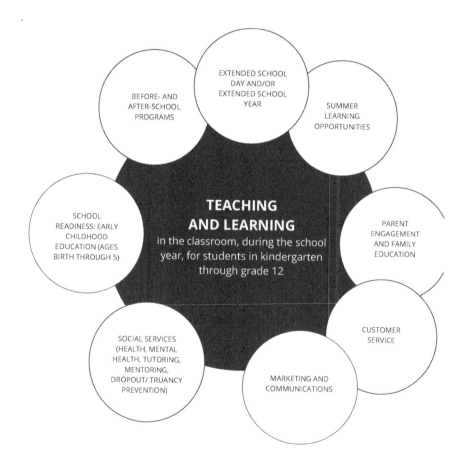

and priority, I took an inelegant stab, showing him an illustration of how teaching and learning could be seen as not only connected to marketing and communications, but also to other components of education that I knew mattered to him, all of which needed attention and resources in order to accelerate our progress in closing the achievement gap.

That conversation helped me figure out how to get Superintendent Payzant on board with the idea of promoting the schools through the Y/BPS initiative. He said he needed to know that funds for marketing the schools wouldn't detract from the classroom and that the work of marketing wouldn't detract from the emphasis on teaching and learning. He did eventually allow for the pilot of this new outreach effort, after I assured him that the funds to pilot Y/BPS would come from outside sources and not the school system, and that external partners — from City Hall to local nonprofits — would share in the challenge of marketing the schools.

6. VIEW AMBIVALENCE AS A PART OF THE PROCESS, BUT NOT A PLACE TO LAND PERMANENTLY.

"It is difficult to roll up one's sleeves and get to work, if we are stuck wringing our hands." -Hillary Clinton, *It Takes a Village*

Parenting in general, and the reality of mothers working, is a place where Clinton's quote hits the mark. *Should mothers work?* is an example of the silly questions we're stuck on. Our country has spent decades debating if mothers should work, while other countries, knowing women *will* choose and/or *need* to work, long ago put in place affordable and high-quality childcare and elder care. Here, in some circles, we still demonize middle-income women who choose to work outside the home as selfish, because they spend less time with their children, while demonizing low-income mothers who *don't* work outside the home (who work full-time as mothers) as lazy.

Should women rise up the ladder in the workplace, or does the workplace need to be changed to allow for both men and women to live balanced lives and actually see their children? Is the goal really that women climb in higher numbers, working 50–70 hours per week, or that men and women are considered to be loyal, talented, ambitious, productive, creative professionals when they work 30- or 40-hour weeks, allowing for healthier marriages, healthier children, and healthier individuals? You can see my opinion coming through here. I realize many positions are not do-able in 30 hours per week but require 40 to 60, like in some fields of increasing competition and global interactions. But why are we so reticent about the kind of job-shares that would allow two highly talented people (men or women) each to work 30 hours, for a total of a 60-hour position? Efforts to innovate with job-shares and flex time are still too rare.

So that we can avoid landing in permanent ambivalence, let's talk about what it's like to parent in the most difficult circumstances. I remember fleeting conversations in Massachusetts about paying foster parents a full salary, acknowledging that they are performing an excruciatingly hard job — raising other people's children who had to be removed from their birth homes due to abuse or severe neglect. The idea was that to parent these particular kids *did* require someone at home full time and someone with incredible skills, which explained paying a foster parent a salary such as $30,000 or $40,000, arguably a pittance for the 24/7 work required to care for children who suffer from major trauma, with serious, on-going physical and mental ailments.

What was the major resistance to this idea, besides the cost itself? Why wouldn't most state child welfare agencies and nonprofits entertain the idea, even though there is a chronic shortage of foster parents and adoptive parents, and children in the so-called child protection system often end up being further traumatized, bouncing from placement to placement? (And those same damaged young adults have children too young themselves, whom they aren't able to parent well, and the cycle continues.) Advocates abandoned this idea of salaries for foster parents because they had already heard from politicians, who would have to approve the budget changes, that "the wrong kinds of people" would step forward if they got to be paid as full-time foster or adoptive parents — they'd be doing it just for the money, when the work itself should be reward enough. If the work itself should be reward enough, why do we pay police officers or librarians? Or politicians?

So children suffer for our inability to have conversations about how the child welfare system might truly be transformed, with full-time paid foster parents being one possible idea. The farthest advocates have been able to get — and this is actually a big deal — is drawing attention to the travesty of requiring kids in the child welfare system to leave at age 18, if they aren't willing to sign away certain rights. Now, in the majority of states, until they are 21, former foster kids can come back at any point for state guidance and support, even if they initially try to make it on their own at 18.

For five years, once a month I sat in on case reviews of teens in foster care, to help determine if they could safely return home and whether the Department of Social Services was doing enough for them. In every single review of a teen who was aging out of the system, I asked the adults after the kid left the room: How many of us could have made it on our own — to find housing, food, a job — with no family, limited education, a background of abuse, and little money? Why the heck are we expecting kids from tragic circumstances to make it on their own?

Eventually this argument was made by people much more knowledgeable and skilled than I. In this case, leaders in the child welfare system made a decision: we will support foster children at least three years beyond age 18. Identifying ambivalence was a start.

You know, sometimes we learn from our children how natural it is to experience and express ambivalence. At age four, my daughter proclaimed from her bedroom, "I need privacy! I want company!"

Listening with a true intent to understand, admitting what we don't know or are unsure about, welcoming complexity and nuance with a "yes, and…" approach, meeting ambivalent people where they're at, and never allowing ourselves to stay in a place of ambivalence for too long: these steps send us down a path toward new approaches to the complex problems we face.

Chapter 9
THE ANGEL'S IN THE DETAILS

Collaboration (n): an unnatural act
engaged in by consenting adults.
~AUTHOR UNKNOWN

Mindless meetings and poorly crafted coalitions can be the bane of many high-minded organizations and the death of fledgling social justice efforts. Fortunately, conversely, mindful meetings and conscientious coalitions can move mountains.

In 1992, I went to interview for an unusual job that was created by a pair of superheroes. You might not initially cast them as such, our modern-day Batman and Robin. Batman: a pale white woman barely five feet tall, soft features, who carries herself with a reassuring calm, sporting a wavy mop of dark, shoulder-length hair, tinged with gray. An Orthodox Jew, by the way. Her Robin sidekick: an equally modest Black man, medium height, broad grin, peering out at the world behind round spectacles with a quiet wisdom.

Judith Kurland and Ted Landsmark were indeed superheroes, leading the national charge in the early 1990s to think more strategically about how to improve our nation's cities and safeguard their future as the hubs of innovation. Their work grew out of a concern that our country's approach was too narrow regarding such health issues as HIV and AIDS, infant mortality, cancer, and youth dying from violence — as if we could separate out STD transmission, preventable child deaths, the lack of early diagnosis for cancer, and gun murders from the conditions of patients' lives and the conditions of the communities in which they live. Having seen young people and adults thrive in the most difficult of circumstances, they wanted to lift up the thinking about resilience. They asked: What strengths and assets of individuals and communities can be better harnessed to address these crises, especially urban crises?

Kurland was serving as Boston's commissioner of health and hospitals, the first woman to be appointed to this position. She would later go on to be appointed the regional director of health and human services under President Clinton. In 1991, she tapped Landsmark to help her launch a citywide initiative called Healthy Boston. Landsmark's career had taken him to many victories as a lawyer and then government leader. He was perhaps most known for appearing in a Pulitzer Prize-winning photo, the subject of an assault at City Hall Plaza back when Boston grappled with race riots over court-ordered busing to integrate the public schools. The photo shows a few dozen white people rushing around a Black man in a three-piece suit. A white man is rushing toward Landsmark, holding the American flag as a spear to attack him.

> IN 1992, I WENT TO INTERVIEW FOR AN UNUSUAL JOB THAT WAS CREATED BY A PAIR OF SUPERHEROES.

Kurland and Landsmark launched the Healthy Boston initiative with this statement: "Healthy people and healthy communities require more than medical care. They require jobs that can support a family with dignity, decent housing, and enough food to eat. They require quality education that opens the door to opportunity. They require safe, thriving neighborhoods where people help each other."

What would happen, it was posited, if we redefined "health" to include, among other areas, education, housing, public safety — and brought a broader group of players to the table to address and promote health?

With support from then-Mayor Ray Flynn, they announced that any neighborhood could form a coalition to apply for a $60,000 planning grant, which would be followed by up to $250,000 to begin implementation, should the community present an ambitious and yet concrete plan to improve its health. The planning grant would come with a number of conditions, including that the major sectors of the neighborhood, which rarely worked together or even knew each other, had to participate in the planning, from parents to business leaders, health care providers to community centers. And every coalition formed would meet monthly with the other similarly funded neighborhoods, to learn from one another.

So in September of 1992, at age 30, I entered the room for my job interview with one of these newly forming Healthy Boston Coalitions, feeling prepared and calm. To be honest, I wasn't nervous because I was skeptical. As a community organizer turned project manager who had stepped out of the workforce to earn a graduate degree in management (with lots of student debt hanging over me), why would I want to run a rag-tag coalition with a vague mission? But it's always good practice to go to an interview.

Little did I know that the interview committee of 15 — representing social service agencies, a neighborhood bank, the YMCA, a hospital, and a local health center — didn't expect me to be a good fit either. Most doubted they would end up hiring an outsider from across town to run their first-ever neighborhood-wide convening. They felt proud of and protective of their community, Allston-Brighton, one of the largest city neighborhoods and the most ethnically diverse, where more than 21 languages were spoken. I, they pointed out, spoke only English fluently, plus some Spanish and sign language. And I had never lived in Allston-Brighton.

It wasn't love at first sight, but it was surely intrigue and respect at first introduction. During the interview, I shared my views about where community organizing and nonprofit management coincided, and what it might take to bring everyone out to identify the common challenges in the neighborhood — to make this touchy-feely-sounding initiative concrete for community members. I spoke of effective and inclusive planning meetings alongside immediate and visible change, such as neighbors banding together to ensure the towing of abandoned cars that create blight and invite crime.

The mix of people in the room blew me away with their intelligence and passion. A tall, gracious nun spoke of her convent's work to expand access to English as a Second Language programs. A couple nonprofit directors expressed concern about how to expand programming for teenagers, given the mild competition between organizations, the growing complexity of the youth population (now from many home countries), and limited funds. The head of the senior center and the president of a local bank spoke about the challenges of breaking down barriers between long-time elderly Irish citizens and the Mexican and Iranian "newcomers" who had lived in the neighborhood for years.

Building on that theme, a beautiful white-haired woman in her 70s, who belonged to a church now filled with immigrant families, explained how much she loved the neighborhood. Her husband was urging her to move to a warmer climate and less expensive location, but she refused to retire until the team assembled had figured out a way to address, and ideally prevent, emerging racial and cultural tensions. The essence of feisty and unbowed, having survived multiple bouts of breast cancer, this woman announced that her work in life was not done. This new coalition inspired her.

It hit me: this was a neighborhood with as much diversity — racial, age, ethnic, socioeconomic — as one could find literally anywhere in the world. And it was a neighborhood on the edge. Fears about crime were increasing, and the social service safety nets couldn't keep up with emerging needs, yet the neighborhood overall was still relatively calm, safer than other areas of Boston. We could explore *prevention* here, rather than crisis intervention.

I survived that first coalition interview, and they eventually offered me the position after realizing that no one coming to work in Allston-Brighton would speak all 21 languages of the neighborhood, and perhaps an "outsider" might bring the objectivity and skills needed to bring people together. I would report to the director of the neighborhood community center, who affectionately dubbed me General Sherman, offering me a small office and a good salary. I signed on, learning hearty lessons about meetings and coalitions in those four years.

We reviewed census data; surveyed all 35 health and social service organizations; interviewed 45 individuals representing different sectors, business to higher ed; held focus groups with business leaders and with residents, young and old, in Vietnamese, Haitian Creole, Chinese, English, and Spanish; and hosted open monthly meetings to continuously share and shape the needs assessment.

The opportunity to do this prevention work got me up every morning, eager to get to the coalition office. Tenant organizers were meeting with hospital executives now; white senior citizens were brainstorming with Vietnamese teenagers; elementary school principals were talking with affordable housing developers.

Our community assessment process identified four priorities shared across the neighborhood:

1. The need for more English as a Second Language and Adult Basic Education services. (The wait list at one agency alone was 500 adults.)

2. A deep concern about access to health and social services for low-income people, people of color, and immigrant residents. (For example, infant mortality rates were higher for black infants, and access to prenatal care was much lower for many mothers of color than for white mothers in the same income bracket.)

3. A lack of afterschool and job readiness activities for teenagers.

4. A growing concern about neighborhood safety and cohesiveness.

Based on the report, several neighborhood institutions made immediate changes in their procedures, such as offering more transportation and translation services. Other organizations put aside competition to collaborate more effectively on youth needs, raising funds as partners, and offering more nighttime activities, guided by a multiracial group of teenagers who signed on to become a neighborhood advisory board. And religious groups began to train volunteers to meet the need for English coaching, while the community developed a more sustainable adult education funding plan.

Throughout the planning process, our coalition and the 20 others in the city met regularly and received technical assistance from the central Healthy Boston team. Commissioner Kurland had hired Landsmark and another professional named Jerry Mogul to manage the citywide network of 21 Healthy Boston neighborhood initiatives. Those three helped me cut my teeth on running complex meetings and building unlikely coalitions, as I turned to them often for support. A year into the work, Landsmark and Mogul announced that the Allston-Brighton Coalition was the only one ready to receive the initial round of quarter-million-dollar implementation grants.

To this day, some two decades after I left the coalition to work in City Hall, I continue to reflect on what we did there, and how hard (and important) it is to run effective meetings and sustain a broad coalition.

When the agenda is fighting the good fight, it's all too easy for us to forget the basics, to think the importance of the work will preordain success, resulting in meetings that falter and coalitions that crumble. The devil of a problem for many organizations and coalitions is simply a lack of intentionality, which is perhaps the theme in much of our faltering work: we need not only *follow-through*, but, more important, we need *forethought*.

> WHEN THE AGENDA IS FIGHTING THE GOOD FIGHT, IT'S ALL TOO EASY FOR US TO FORGET THE BASICS, TO THINK THE IMPORTANCE OF THE WORK WILL PREORDAIN SUCCESS, RESULTING IN MEETINGS THAT FALTER AND COALITIONS THAT CRUMBLE.

We find ourselves gathering in a room that's so hot the group is wilting, or running a meeting where a small portion of the members do all the talking and important ideas go unsaid by people who are more reserved. We begin the work of a coalition before making sure all the key players have been invited, later surprised at how many people we've alienated, or try to operate a coalition without staff, only to find the group falling apart after nine months. I know; I've been there, and made mistakes. And more mistakes. Fortunately, I've had mentors and colleagues who have given me feedback along the way, sometimes feedback I asked for, sometimes unsolicited advice that made me cringe at the moment, but also made me a better activist. I wish I could say I always remember and follow this advice, but it's still a struggle in a busy workplace.

When I think of the importance of mindful meetings, it's bemusing to reflect on one particular period of my time in city government. The mid- and senior-level staff gathered monthly from every department within health, education, and human services. It was a superb team, with the goal of improving communication, coordination, and collaboration across the silos of city government.

So we all met together . . . in a dungeon. Seriously. Well, there were no handcuffs from which to hang people, and actually it was called the Bunker. After 9/11, this room was created so the mayor and his team could have a safe place to convene and run the city in the event of a terrorist attack. Located in the basement of City Hall, the Bunker had no windows and featured all kinds of cool gadgets, screens, buttons. Interesting place to tour; not such a productive place to hold monthly two-hour meetings. Every four weeks, 25 of us squeezed into this dank, depressing space. The center table only sat about 15, so a second circle formed around the perimeter, meaning everyone in the room either had their back to someone else, or looked at a colleague's behind. Thank goodness at some point a wise new assistant to our chief of staff moved us upstairs to a new room.

That was almost as comically un-mindful as the time, a few years later, when 28 of us from my temple met at a Sunday workshop to discuss what "relational Judaism" might mean for our congregation. That term "relational" refers to infusing any mission-driven organization with an understanding that every member, new and old, needs to know other people and be known in order for the organization to thrive. The urgency of this concept was becoming clear across many Jewish synagogues; a major Pew foundation report interviewing American Jews had indicated decreasing interest in temples, since there are so many other places in our lives where we can live out our Judaism — at home, in a community center — if the temple doesn't feel like home.

Ours is a huge temple building, with an equally large membership (1,000 families), so a member can feel lonely or alienated without an intentional focus on relationships. The workshop leader offered up fascinating stories and concrete examples of revitalized temples. Funny thing was that no one who organized the meeting thought to have the attendees introduce ourselves and get connected before the leader began his talk. Or to get to know each other at any point during the meeting. The assumption was we all had existing strong relationships. Many of us left this meeting on relationships not knowing some of the people in the room from our own congregation. Oops.

My friends in the business world regale me with tales of being in mandatory meetings where everyone is so bored they pretend to be taking notes on their phone, but are really scanning online for holiday bargains. Or a senior executive puts slides up stuffed with text and proceeds to read each word on the slide to his audience. So the lack of mindfulness doesn't take place simply in the nonprofit, public, or activist spheres.

Mindful, in this case, is another word for intentional. We've got to know *why* we're meeting, and make sure our meetings achieve the goal in a way that continues to build effective working relationships among the participants.

When I worked in the mayor's office, one day we might be convening a team of college presidents to talk about the impact of student drinking on families in those neighborhoods, and the next day bringing together elderly couples who had been married for 50 years to share their successes with young couples. We might bring together health care providers around the infant mortality crisis or brainstorm with St. Patrick's Day parade organizations how and why to allow an LGBT veterans' group to march in their event. Or we might be meeting quietly with a few small nonprofits to understand how to help them merge and thus continue to serve their clients.

A.P.R. IS MY GUIDING ACRONYM, A REMINDER OF THE IMPORTANCE OF THE BEFORE, THE DURING, AND THE AFTER OF A MEETING: ATTENDANCE (GET THE RIGHT PEOPLE IN THE ROOM); PRODUCTIVITY (ENSURE THE MEETING IS A SUPERB USE OF THEIR TIME); AND RESULTS (BE CLEAR WHAT THE GOAL IS, AND WHAT NEEDS TO HAPPEN AFTER THE MEETING TO MEET THOSE GOALS).

Every meeting is different, but some key principles enhance success. A.P.R. is my guiding acronym — a reminder of the importance of the before, the during, and the after of a meeting: Attendance (get the right people in the room); Productivity (ensure the meeting is a superb use of their time); and Results (be clear what the goal is, and what needs to happen after the meeting to meet those goals).

ATTENDANCE

Ensuring meeting attendance, especially if the group or coalition is new, can require those three points of contact I've talked about: reach out to the participant via technology, a print resource, and a phone call. It might seem excessive, since now we synch our calendars online, and a ping on a smartphone will give us a reminder of the upcoming meeting. But if it doesn't feel like an urgent gathering to that person, and isn't mandated by their workplace, they can dismiss the ping with a swipe, or not bother to put it on their calendars in the first place.

Are there people you really need in the room? Send a personalized email, and ideally ask for a proactive one-line RSVP response that is more than hitting "okay." Include a sentence that invites an actual response, such as, "Please confirm that you will attend, and list one item you would like to see on the agenda." Follow up with a phone call to those who don't respond to the email. They need to know their participation matters. And they need to take some small step to respond to you that will make them feel accountable for coming and for being an active participant when they show up.

In the Allston-Brighton Healthy Boston Coalition, the steering committee made a list of all the different constituencies in the neighborhood: cultural groups underrepresented at meetings, such as Cambodians; leaders not at the table, such as tenant groups; corporate partners, such as banks. We divvied up who knew whom and might be able to bring a new member to the next meeting. At the end of each meeting, we did the same with the assembled group. Soon more than 100 people were gathering monthly to frame and participate in the neighborhood-wide planning.

PRODUCTIVITY

A few simple steps dramatically increase the effectiveness and productivity during a meeting, and thus the likelihood that members will return:

1. *Pay attention to logistics.* That includes atmosphere. Too hot is the death of creativity, and windows make a difference. Seating matters; no one should be in an outer circle unless you

intend to make a statement about lack of importance. And do you want tables set up to break into small group discussion? Pay attention to food, with just enough to keep their energy up and create an atmosphere where people will chat during a break. Poster paper, markers, slides, thumb-drives — is everything there and is all audio-visual tested to make sure it works? Choose locations that can accommodate people with mobility issues. Make sure there is interpretation for non-English speakers. Is the location accessible by public transportation? Check the calendar for religious holidays.

2. *Engage from the start.* Open in a way that interests the members, so they are primed to pay attention and participate, rather than doze off. When we engage the mind, we increase productivity; and when we engage the body, we engage the mind — so it can help simply to get people to move. Depending on the group, it often does work to use a warm-up exercise, but done in a way that is not experienced as touchy-feely. "Stand Up, Sit Down" works well, and can take just two minutes: "Stand up if you speak more than one language." (Everyone then sits back down.) "Stand up if you play an instrument." "Stand up if you have read a book in the past two months that you couldn't put down. Great, there are six of you. Call out the book titles if you think others might enjoy that read." Heck, if the meeting isn't as productive as you like, everyone will at least leave inspired to add to their reading list. "Stand up if you hate this type of warm-up exercise" always draws a good laugh. If there are people in the room with mobility impairments, raising hands can substitute for standing up.

   If the members know each other and you simply want to wake them up for a post-lunch meeting, especially if there are colleagues you'd like to see working more closely together across departments or organizations, keep it simple with, "Go to someone in the room you have worked with for over a year; find out two things you did not know about them."

   Or a fast one: "As we go around with quick introductions,

heading into winter, what is one strategy you use to survive and enjoy the cold weather?" Who knew Keith runs snow-shoeing races or Sonia organizes potlucks every month of the winter for neighboring households? Saundra and Sachuko, meeting for the first time at this neighborhood organizing effort, both play tennis and are looking for a new teammate. Cool.

3. *Announce a clear purpose and agenda.* Posting the goals on the wall or a smartboard, especially if the group composes the goals together, can head off later acrimony. Posting or handing out the agenda, with times next to each item (Brainstorm about [topic X] 2:45–3:15 p.m.) will keep the group focused and accountable.

4. *Establish ground rules.* Especially if it's a difficult group or a controversial topic, but really for almost any type of meeting, ground rules are helpful. My two favorite ground rules are:

   - *NOSTUESO (No-one Speaks Thrice Until Everyone Speaks Once).* I first heard this from community organizer and facilitator, Julia Ojeda. Speaking once in a meeting is okay; sometimes it's okay to make it twice, as limiting every member to *one* comment is rigid and counterproductive, and some members do have more experience and expertise to offer. But when one member speaks *three times* before other members have spoken even *once*, usually it means that introverted types are not being tapped for their brains, and extroverted types may be speaking for the sake of hearing themselves talk. Once this is set as a ground rule, it makes it easy to come back to the principle toward the end of the meeting: "Is there anyone who hasn't spoken in this second half of the meeting and has an opinion to share before we vote?" or "As we begin to wrap up the meeting, for those of you who have been quieter today, is there something that you might later regret not bringing up about this project? Every insight is needed for us to tackle this problem."

- *Brainstorming is not barnstorming.* Distinguish between the idea-generation stage of the meeting (if there is one) and the discussion, debate, and evaluation phase. Often the facilitator is looking for ideas, trying to open the conversation and hear multiple reactions to a proposal. "We're brainstorming now, just throwing out ideas, not commenting on each other's suggestions here." Without this reminder, it's human nature; as soon as one person makes a statement that is at all controversial, the next member will respond and an entire conversation will become a debate, respectful or not, about the first idea, bringing the idea-generation to a halt.

5. *Be intentional about the presence of technology.* As we have more and more handheld options for distractions in meetings, it helps to be clear about group expectations, rather than avoiding the issue. Is this a time to turn off smartphones or is it fine for members to be texting during the meeting? Are laptops out for note-taking? Is this a long enough meeting where it makes sense to break every 60 to 90 minutes for people to check emails and texts, while taking bathroom breaks and grabbing some fruit and coffee? If so, can the group agree to turn off all electronics until those scheduled breaks? Note though that in some cases, technology can be an issue of accessibility.

    And if you or another presenter uses technology to advance the meeting content, be quite intentional about practicing beforehand and not having the images replace a skillful presentation. Slides, for example, should augment the presentation, not *be* the presentation. A great short video clip can change up a meeting fabulously. Slides packed with words that are recited by the presenter kill a meeting.

6. *Review to agree.* At the end of a meeting, review out loud the decisions made and next steps. Often, I find that in fact people did not agree on something we thought was consensus,

or there may be two follow-up tasks that no one has owned.

7. *Evaluate the meeting — briefly.* What worked well in terms of logistics and substance? (You may be surprised.) What would improve the group's functioning? ("Next time when you send us these excellent materials to read in advance, I'd prefer you assume we have read them and can start right into the conversation, rather than taking 20 minutes to review the content.") And be direct about soliciting feedback. I have found people are more likely to return to the next meeting when I ask, "Was this worth 90 minutes of your time? And if not, and the work is important to you, what would make it completely worth your time at the next meeting?"

8. *Be selective about scheduling meetings.* When setting future meetings, determine how many more meetings this group actually needs to accomplish the goals.

9. *Change it up.* If the group *does* need to continue gathering, there is no reason the format must remain consistent. When I am meeting one-on-one with someone, and there is no reason for extensive note-taking, we usually discuss the topic while walking outside for 45 minutes. Ideas flow much more rapidly when we are moving — it works even better than caffeine. Alternate the location of board meetings, especially if it provides an opportunity for the board to see a component of the program in action.

10. *Make sure meetings reflect the mission.* Conduct meetings in a way that reflects and furthers the work. Playworks is a great example. It is a national nonprofit that helps schools "energize education" by recovering learning time for teachers and also focusing on reducing bullying. They provide coaches throughout the school day, to run sports during recess and after school and to help teachers incorporate physical activity into traditional academic subjects, as well as teaching older students to manage games and activities with younger kids. I was on the Playworks board, where the executive director started every meeting with some sort of physical activity that

also helped us understand what went on in Playworks schools. "This is marathon week in the city, so the letter of the day is M. Stand up and touch four items in the room that start with M — and if it happens to be Manuel or Miranda, keep the touching to their shoulder, please," he'd say. He would then explain, "We tell teachers that if their students seem stuck, not understanding a math concept, or simply restless, they can touch four items that begin with M, as quickly as possible, creating mayhem that can feel joyous; then, have them calculate what four items touched, times 21 students, equals. Math on the move!"

For the large Allston-Brighton Healthy Boston Coalition meetings, advertised to the entire community to give input on the needs assessment, we did a couple things uncommon in the 1990s. First, we provided a full dinner to everyone who came, even after the gatherings grew to 100 participants. This served to increase attendance, made for a productive meeting (we could begin right at 6 p.m. without hungry participants), and set an example for exposure to cultural differences because a different ethnic food was served each month. How did we pay for it? We asked a different restaurant each time to provide the food for free, in return for being thanked out loud and in print. No restaurant was asked more than once every two years. Not only did different participants experience a neighborhood restaurant, they got to know something of other cultures present in their area when they'd try Cambodian and Vietnamese fare, Mexican dishes, Irish pub food, Chinese or Indian meals.

The meetings took place around the neighborhood, anywhere there was a large enough room — the local elementary school, St. Elizabeth's Hospital, a meeting space at Boston College. We always set up a round table structure, 6 or 8 or 10 to a table, so that some part of each meeting could be participatory. A small team of neighborhood residents, business leaders, elected officials, and service providers chose the topics for the monthly meetings, and we tried to keep everyone in and outside the coalition on their toes with varying topics and formats — all in service of this broader issue of community health. Because the issue *was* such a broad one, and because by nature, coalitions convene those who are not used to working together, at every meeting we posted the vision and mission of the coalition, one laminated sign in each of the 12 major languages spoken. And we always reviewed the recent successes and activities of the coalition in the first few minutes, after an introductory exercise. This addressed the common problem of newcomers arriving at a meeting unsure of the bigger purpose of the group. Every meeting included not just time for relationship-building and report-backs on committee work, but also substantive content on an issue that members had voted on as important to them.

My favorite coalition meeting was the one where a woman originally from Mexico came up to talk to me after. She said she had immigrated 10 years earlier, but it wasn't until the creation of the coalition that she felt she could call the neighborhood home.

RESULTS

The two most important post-meeting actions are:

1. *Send a <u>brief</u> summary to participants.* Detailed notes are not noteworthy to most people. While technology, from email to Dropbox, makes it easier than ever to send out meeting notes, does anyone read them? Keep them in case there is a problem to be addressed later, but for participants, simply send a summary of major decisions made and who is responsible for each next step. If I need to ensure that this summary has been read (because the next steps are particularly urgent), I ask people to reply via email that they received and reviewed the decisions, and to click whether they agree with what was stated. My latest approach to "minutes" is to write up on a whiteboard the decisions and next steps from the meeting, review the whiteboard notes with everyone as the meeting is winding down, take a photo, and send it to all participants. Done.

2. *Engage the absentees.* If someone important to the team has missed a meeting, ask a meeting member to call her and review the major decisions. I will often ask at the beginning of a meeting for three people to volunteer to call the three absen-

tees, which tends to ensure the volunteers engage more in the meeting, in order to report it.

One of the more potent Healthy Boston meetings focused on crime, with voices raised and everyone speaking up. Again, it's all about relationships. The goal was for the neighborhood's new police captain — the first woman in that role — to meet this diverse group of neighborhood residents. She presented an overview of crime statistics in the neighborhood and the plans to prevent and deal with crime. We then asked people to discuss at their own table how safe they felt in the neighborhood and why — and to list, if they were willing, any crimes they had seen or experienced that had gone unreported for any reason, including fear of reporting. The meeting helped the residents put a face to the names of officers they had not met, and provided the captain with a deeper understanding of what might be happening in the community unbeknownst to the officers, from car break-ins that went unreported to concerns about domestic violence for immigrants afraid they would be deported for speaking up.

Sometimes the meetings stood on their own and needed no particular follow-up; other times the participants decided the topic warranted a six-month project, such as when a group formed to look at better coordination of smoking cessation programs.

Operating an effective coalition includes some of the same principles as running effective meetings: be proactive and intentional, operate in a way that reinforces the mission, encourage relationships, and revere (and reinforce) results.

Here are my principles for creating effective coalitions:

1. *Define success.* Remember how tough it is for busy people to make coalition work a priority, so help them stay focused, and make sure the coalition meets their needs. By its nature, a coalition is an added responsibility. For someone working at United Way, a coalition of youth-serving organizations may help her address a serious unmet need in the community, as the team plans for expanded hunger relief programming, but

she already has a full plate at her job. She wonders if this new coalition will really advance the issue, or just make for more meetings. Ask at the start: "Please fill in this sentence: 'This new work will have been worth it, if one year from now _____ has happened.'" Put all the answers together on the wall for every coalition meeting.

2. *Staff the coalition.* One of the biggest mistakes when forming a new group is to think that the mission is so energizing that the members can pull it off on top of their current responsibilities, or with a very part-time person overseeing it. Someone has to be focused on the coalition itself, I have found, for the work to be high-enough quality to meet its goals, and for the group to function in a way that isn't, well, dysfunctional. At the Allston-Brighton Coalition, they weren't trying to build another nonprofit, but staffed it with me as a director, two very impressive graduate student interns each year, and pulled in full-time staff people for periods of time when we were launching a major new project, before the project could be folded into an existing organization.

3. *Tackle substantive challenges.* Choose at least one meaty piece of work to conduct together, right from the start, to determine whether the coalition is truly needed and will be truly useful.

4. *Also choose low-hanging fruit.* While more complicated work is planned, coalition members must create relationships and see progress. In Allston-Brighton, we needed to raise funds, so we developed a community-wide nomination process for unsung heroes, culminating in a public event with live entertainment to honor them. It was a simple idea, and applauding unsung heroes was certainly not a new one. Yet we thought that in a place as wildly diverse as Allston-Brighton, we would be able to honor at least one teen each year for peer leadership, one or more adult long-time residents, and one or more immigrants from undervalued or simply unknown groups. In other words, we could raise funds while bringing together people

who almost never interacted in the community, people unaware that groups culturally different from themselves even
lived there. The first year of this unsung heroes event, the audience of 200 was deeply moved by the story of a woman who
had survived the killing fields in Cambodia, where she lost
her husband, then came to the Allston-Brighton community
to create mental health services for other refugees. She was
honored alongside lifelong residents of the neighborhood,
including Irish Catholic twin sisters in their 80s who volunteered to visit other elders. The people who had most resisted
the creation of the coalition in the first place came out to
honor their friends and decided to take a second look at the
work we were undertaking.

I have participated in, and learned from, many an effective meeting and many a ground-breaking coalition. It's inspiring, knowing that
a passionate group can improve the conditions in a community or elect
forward-thinking candidates. Truth be told, I always have, and still do,
look forward to most meetings I attend. I always thought it was a good
thing until I read:

> *"People who enjoy meetings should not be in charge of anything."*
> ~Thomas Sowell

So, from someone who clearly should not be in charge of anything,
I suggest, for productive sessions that advance your work:
- Pay close attention to logistics.
- Activate everyone.
- Announce a clear purpose and agenda.
- Establish ground rules.
- Review decisions.
- Evaluate the meeting — briefly.
- Be selective about scheduling further meetings.
- Change up the experience.
- Use a structure that reflects and reinforces the mission.

Chapter 10

LEVELING THE SANDBOX

"It is easier to build strong children
than to fix broken men."
~FREDERICK DOUGLASS

As I move toward the end of this book, I want to focus on the beginning — of our lives, and of our movements. We spend so much time and expend so many resources trying to remediate situations we could have prevented, from economic inequities to physical illnesses, from climate change to a housing shortage. Prevention and forethought are too often an afterthought.

Working to stem the AIDS epidemic was my first exposure to the importance of prevention over intervention. Then my work on early childhood policy for Mayor Menino reinforced the power of prevention. The early childhood work also afforded an opportunity to practice the lessons I've explored throughout this book.

There is great joy in working on issues facing young children and their families. Kids are often best at reminding us what's right and what's real, as Maurice Sendak, acclaimed author of *Where the Wild Things Are*, revealed in a 2011 interview with NPR's Terry Gross:

GROSS: Can you share some of your favorite comments from readers that you've gotten over the years?
SENDAK: Oh, there's so many. Can I give you just one that I really like? It was from a little boy. He sent me a charming card with a little drawing. I loved it. I answer all my children's letters

— sometimes very hastily — but this one I lingered over. I sent him a postcard and I drew a picture of a Wild Thing on it. I wrote "Dear Jim, I loved your card." Then I got a letter back from his mother and she said, "Jim loved your card so much he ate it." That to me was one of the highest compliments I've ever received. He didn't care that it was an original drawing or anything. He saw it, he loved it, he ate it.

The science of early childhood teaches us a great deal about the justice behind prevention work for many crucial issues.

Imagine the sudden crash of thunder outside your bedroom window, shocking you out of a deep sleep. The rapid-fire POW! POW! POW! of fireworks you hadn't known were going to be released the night before July 4th, causing your pulse to accelerate. The way your heart rate increases if a colleague unexpectedly confronts you in a meeting. The tightening in your chest when, walking four blocks to the subway late at night, someone brushes against your sleeve — the tension that

PREVENTION AND FORETHOUGHT ARE TOO OFTEN AN AFTERTHOUGHT.

builds before you realize he means no harm. The anxiety when the call comes, informing you that the job for which you had been a finalist went to someone else, panic emerging that you won't be able to provide for your family.

What happens in the human body during these times? A chemical called cortisol floods the brain, kicking in a normal fight-or-flight reaction, providing you with adrenaline in case you must either engage in battle or flee. Once you realize you are okay, the systems in your body return to a normal state. It's just fireworks, you realize. Or thunder. The stranger brushed you by accident.

If it takes longer to determine you are safe, or you are *not* safe, your system stays on alert, the cortisol levels remaining high. If you are hearing the POW and are not sure whether it is fireworks or a gunshot. If the person confronting you isn't a colleague at a meeting, but a partner who showers you daily at home with condemnation, anger, and the threat of physical harm. If the person brushing by *does* mean harm, his gesture a warning that you've encroached on his turf. The cortisol floods your system for longer, remains high, your body begins to be worn down.

That is what happens to the *adult* system. What about a child's body, if they face serious threat early on, when the brain is undergoing its greatest time of development, when the immune system is forming, when memory and the brain's ability to absorb new information is being created, when the synapses on which the brain relies are literally being formed, destroyed, or left to wither? The threat to a child could be watching their father hit their mother. Having to move from home to home because parents fear violence or don't have enough for rent.

Neuroscience now documents that the child under constant siege will have an immune system and brain that form differently than those of other babies, toddlers, and preschoolers who live in safe and stable environments. The formation of memory, the basis of the ability to learn, is hindered. And the normal, healthy, fight-or-flight reflex necessary in all human beings will become hair-trigger; as the child grows older, it will kick in too quickly, too often, and fail to recede appropriately, giving the child (who becomes a young adult, then an adult) the sense that risk is present even when it is not.

The terms for this range of experiences are *normal stress* (what every child should and does feel, such as the disappointment when she can't have something she wants, or the challenge of learning a new task); *tolerable stress* (challenges to safety or development — even as serious as short-term homelessness or the loss of a parent to cancer — that are buffered by the existence of one or more stable, nurturing, safe adults in the child's life); and *toxic stress* (when the threats are constant, severe, unmitigated). We now know that when cortisol and other chemicals rise in a young child and remain high for long periods of time, it impacts the very architecture of the brain and the very development of the immune system. There are all kinds of troubling implications, from a teenage boy who sees a simple glance at his girlfriend as a threat and feels justified in pulling a knife (his fight-or-flight response is set to go off too easily), to an adult who has developed heart disease as a result of an immune system that never fully formed.

To be clear, experts in this field of neuroscience aren't arguing that a child's experience in the first five years of life dooms her. What early threats do, though, is create a fragile brain architecture and a fragile health system in place of a resilient one. What happens to young children when their brains are developing most rapidly in those first few years predicts — with eerie accuracy — what their health status and educational attainment will be as they move through life.

For decades, scientists and economists have demonstrated the value of interventions in the earliest years of a child's life, preventing (or quickly halting) exposure to toxic stress. In other words, the most efficient and cost-effective means of closing the academic achievement gap is to prevent the gap from opening in the first place.

The old adage when one is buying a home or opening a business is to focus on where it is situated: location, location, location. It's time we get equally as repetitive in our justice lexicon: prevention, prevention, prevention.

Beyond the biological research that supports focusing on the earliest years of life, there is just plain justice. One can't

> THE MOST EFFICIENT AND COST-EFFECTIVE MEANS OF CLOSING THE ACADEMIC ACHIEVEMENT GAP IS TO PREVENT THE GAP FROM OPENING IN THE FIRST PLACE.

pull herself up by her boots straps if she has no boots. None of us can reach our potential in life with constant barriers put in front of us — the kind that are persistent, weighty, and dangerous. As I noted when talking about class size inequities, what kind of magic are we expecting teachers to perform if they have a room of 35 students, whereas their peers in another setting teach 12 kids? How can the kids in that first classroom reach their full potential?

While justice should be the main reason we care about all children, I am glad to see that some of our country's champions of early education and parental support are top economists who can also quantify the return on investment. These include Art Rolnick, former director of research at the Federal Reserve Bank of Minneapolis, and Nobel Laureate James J. Heckman, professor at the University of Chicago. They note that preventive measures save tremendous resources we currently invest in remediation; preventive measures also build our base of taxpayers, as more people are well prepared to enter the workforce. The return on investment for high-quality early childhood work — excellent preschool provided to children living in poverty, combined with home visiting to strengthen and support parenting — is apparent in real dollars, saving $8.60 for every dollar spent.[1]

From Neurons to Neighborhoods, a groundbreaking publication commissioned by the National Academy of Science in 2000, compiled research on the health impacts of early childhood experiences. One of the authors, Jack P. Shonkoff, provided scientific guidance to our Thrive in 5 school readiness initiative. Mayor Menino approved the creation of the Thrive in 5 movement based on the scientific and economic imperative of focusing on the early years of children's lives, combined with the moral imperative he believed in strongly, which reflects one of our country's basic principles: every child should have an opportunity to reach his or her potential.

This is why I recommended to Mayor Menino that he begin using the term "leveling the sandbox" in his speeches. When kids get to be school-age, many move onto the playing field — soccer, basketball, baseball. But what about their earlier play spaces? When our afterschool programs have to focus on remediation versus enrichment, we are forfeiting points. When a child receives special education services in *grade* three to manage autism that went undiagnosed at *age* three, we are coming late to the field.

The groundwork for the achievement gap — differences in academic performance by economic or racial/cultural group — is laid long before kids enter school. Studies reveal that young people from middle- and upper-income homes develop a vocabulary before they enter kindergarten light years ahead of that demonstrated by their low-income and poor peers. My colleague Robert Wadsworth from the Boston Foundation once said that trying to learn to read and write words in kindergarten, grade one, and grade two that a child has never heard can be almost as hard as learning a new language.

Within the Thrive in 5 movement, one of the most rewarding projects I worked on for the mayor allowed me continually to ask if I was putting into practice these lessons I've captured in *Chasing Social Justice*. It was a TV show called *Parenting in Action.*

During a community meeting with 35 parents, grandparents, and foster parents from across Boston, I asked where they got their information about parenting. The answers were: websites, books, this hotline or that, people they respected at social service organizations. Parents of all cultures in the room noted that they wanted and needed more information and support than they got, often feeling isolated from other parents or having no family. Boston is a relatively small city, and it seemed odd to me that we couldn't provide some sort of basic, coordinated parenting resource.

Mayor Menino cared deeply about making resources available to more people. I thought it would be possible to create such a TV show for very little money, using the city's cable network and a lot of pro bono labor. It turned out I was right: the total invested in the show, beyond in-kind services, was under $75K to produce and air it for three years and then create boxed sets of DVDs, free for long-term use in programs that served parents (back when DVDs were a common and useful tool!).

I asked myself questions to stay focused on what I had learned over the years about power, the effective use of language, the human connection. How could I make sure none of the episodes on the show were polarizing? For example, studies clearly demonstrate that breastfeeding is healthiest for mom and baby and costs significantly less than formula, but we had to present this without demonizing mothers who chose not to (or couldn't) breastfeed. I knew that just creating a good show would *not* mean anyone would watch — if you build it, they still won't come if they don't know about it! How could I make the show relevant for the parents who felt they needed the information most, as making it real makes it possible? Could the show, on an ongoing basis, name the truth that parenting really is the toughest job? How could a TV show build relationships among people who most needed them? What kind of language and terminology should we use? Could the show help stressed parents identify and use their power? How could we reach people beyond those who already were "in the know" about parenting information and city resources? What role should awareness about race and racism play in making the show more effective?

A multicultural focus group of parents and grandparents provided initial guidance. They offered up the topics they wanted to learn about, weighed in on the best time and day to air the show, and gave very important advice: please don't *tell* us what to do — *show* us. They wanted us to *show* the right portion size for healthy eating with little kids; *show* how to manage tantrums. One grandmother in the group agreed. "Yes, yes!" she exclaimed in Spanish. "We need action. Call it *Parenting in Action — Padres en Acción!*" And the title of the show was born. It aired in English and Spanish.

Although I was comfortable on camera, and we could keep project expenses down by the mayor donating my time to host the show, I knew that as a white woman in a city with primarily parents of color, I should not host alone. I reached out to a colleague, Cherie Craft, an African American woman who had landed the Smart from the Start director position a few years earlier. Having grown up in a Boston housing development and then gone on to create highly effective programming for parents breaking cycles of poverty, Cherie knew her stuff. Smart, funny and charismatic, she was the ideal co-host. However, busy with her Smart from the Start work, she could only commit to the initial two episodes, and then helping out sporadically.

Thankfully, for episode number two, Cherie brought on Mireille Louis, a parent from her Smart from the Start program who would serve as a guest expert on the topic of the sandwich generation dilemma — parenting young children while caring for ailing grandparents. Mireille was out of work, raising her five-year-old daughter Arielle as a single parent, while also caring for her Haitian parents who were in their 90s, neither of whom spoke English. Mireille's on-air presence, her wisdom, and her warmth touched me. Mireille accepted the offer to become permanent co-host.

The advisory committee knew *Parenting in Action* couldn't air only on the Boston cable station; it had to have a web presence and eventually be used as a teaching tool with groups of parents, otherwise it would be … well … just for show. We needed to bring the show *to* parents, rather than expecting them to find us. A talented communications student from Boston University created our website and Facebook presence, then tracked our hits and other measures of success. Since the majority of viewers would be Latina and Black parents, one of the standards we developed for the show was that at least 60 percent of our guest experts should be people of color.

It wasn't always easy to stick to another goal — showing, not telling, about parenting — given the limitations of taping the show in a neighborhood cable studio. We worked hard to make it real. For an episode on asthma, we put up a slide that showed a healthy lung next to an asthmatic lung, as a nurse laid out the causes and treatments for asthma, also referring parents to free programs for kids with asthma to stay physically active. In an episode on how parents can do right by their kids even if they have a contentious relationship with their ex, we hosted a Latina teen mom who was no longer with her boyfriend and an African American man in his 40s, divorced from his wife. They each gave specific examples of how they maintain contact with their ex-partner for the benefit of their children. They urged our viewers never to put the child in the middle, even when things are horrible with the co-parent: "Tell yourself daily: I love my child more than I hate my ex."

We kept working hard to make it real. During an episode on maternal depression, viewers saw a role play of a distressed mother asking a relative to take care of her children while she sought treatment. In an episode on expanding children's language in homes where the parents do not know how to read or are not native English speakers, a Korean pediatrician demonstrated how to build storytelling into daily life, as the parent bathes the child, or spends time on the subway or in the grocery store.

Knowing how important language is, for an episode on toddler and preschool behavior, we heard from a pediatrician born in Guatemala and a child psychiatrist from Children's Hospital. These experts urged parents to think beyond punishing and more toward teaching children healthy lessons, using a term called "self-regulation." Mireille and I decided that on all our shows we would require the guests to use more common and easily understood language, but we would also have the experts explain the technical terms, so all of us parents could be exposed to them. Self-regulation was explained as the ability to remember and juggle information; the ability to pay attention; the ability to be flexible in how one thinks; the ability to manage emotions; and the ability to stop and think.

Autism was a topic parents wanted to learn more about. Our guest pediatrician came on to help us through it, sharing that her own child was on the spectrum and describing the range of symptoms and behaviors that, together, indicate that a parent should ask for an evaluation.

In addition to airing it, we wanted to bring the show to parents who could watch it together and share solutions. Through the generosity of an anonymous donor, we were able

AFTER *PARENTING IN ACTION* BEGAN AIRING, UNDERSTANDING THE POWER OF PREVENTION, MAYOR MENINO'S WIFE ANGELA OFFERED TO TOUR EACH NEIGHBORHOOD WITH EXPECTANT MOMS, SO THEY COULD KNOW ABOUT LOCAL RESOURCES BEFORE THE BABY WAS EVEN BORN.

to provide the boxed sets free to programs that committed to use the series with parents — at Head Start programs, in the waiting room of health centers, and through tenant programs at our housing developments. We knew DVDs would eventually become obsolete, so we also posted the most important episodes on YouTube.

Here is something that makes me smile all these years later, as I think about the legacy of Mayor Menino and his family, who taught me so much. After *Parenting in Action* began airing, understanding the power of prevention, Mayor Menino's wife Angela offered to tour each neighborhood with expectant moms, so they could know about local resources before the baby was even born. We asked health care providers working with low-income pregnant women if they would let their patients know about this opportunity to meet the First Lady and learn about neighborhood resources. Groups of up to 10 women would pile into a van to meet one another and Angela. They visited the local library to get a library card, saw where the WIC office was for food and breastfeeding support, and learned where they could get information about childcare, as well as about employment, if they were unemployed or under-employed. They were able to sign up for a parent support group. Some of the women said they wanted to go on, as Mireille my co-host did, to become community leaders helping other parents.

There are many policy arenas in addition to early childhood and family support where the impact of prevention is evident, whether it be affordable housing, climate science, or health care. Any of them warrant a chapter of their own, and that is for another day, someone else's book, hopefully echoing this theme: prevention, prevention, prevention.

The First Lady's neighborhood tours, the *Parenting in Action* show, and most of the early childhood policy work done throughout the city exemplified much of what I have learned through various organizations and movements: make it real to make it possible, prioritize the human connection, create new ways to market, and use our power to open doors so that others can identify their own prowess.

Conclusion
HOW DO WE KEEP ON KEEPING ON?

"The future isn't something we step into;
it is what we create."
~SARA STONE, FORMER PRINCIPAL,
MANNING ELEMENTARY SCHOOL

"Good afternoon from the mayor's hardworking 24-hour hotline team! If your street needs further plowing, call it in to us at 617-635-4500. We answered 3,200 snow emergency calls on Monday, 4,300 on Tuesday, and are on pace to double that number today! The mayor has teams out clearing 850 miles of streets, in addition to hundreds of schools and other buildings, and clearing thousands of fire hydrants and access ramps."

I proudly read that Facebook post during the blizzard of 2015, having worked alongside the author years earlier in City Hall. Julianne Doherty wrote from the Mayor's Office of Neighborhood Services. It captured for me the importance of the human connection — and of keeping it real. Giving details helped humanize the mayor's office and establish a tie to residents, encouraging patience from frustrated Bostonians by sharing the scope of what it takes to work with mother nature. Julianne was one of those city workers I told you about in Chapter 3, working long hours to make sure we did everything possible to improve the lives of all residents, especially those most vulnerable. She felt in her gut, early on in life, that she wanted to make a difference on the local level with her one wild and precious life.

To me, the purpose of life is to live a life of purpose. Our country should always be a place of purpose, a place that continuously pursues justice and equality. As I shared in the introduction, I don't see social justice as a noun. It is a process and a perspective: seeing the potential and humanity in every person, understanding that each of us is inherently equal, and equally worthy. We must ensure people can be safe and take down obstacles that prevent others from a quality of life that allows them to reach their potential. Moving towards a more just society — chasing social justice — is something we do as individuals and in groups, in daily life and via organizations and movements, and through the resources of our government.

At almost every monthly meeting for his department heads and policy advisors, Mayor Menino firmly reminded us: our job is to improve the lives of all of Boston's citizens, especially those most vulnerable. For him, government really was of, by, and for the people. I miss working for him, and I miss the man. Boston's longest-serving mayor, Tom Menino, died at 71, just eight months after stepping down from his post.

Thinking of Tom Menino, I realize how sad it is that the norm now seems to be to assume the worst of people looking to serve in elected office, and how cynical we've become about government overall. Many have the notion that taxes are a waste, government either mismanages our money or, worse, steals it; and anyone who relies on government support is lazy. This attitude comes in part from the continued mythology in the US of rugged individualism. Certainly, it didn't help that my generation grew up in the shadow of Vietnam and then Watergate. And of course today, in 2020, we are dealing with a national leader, enabled by his political party, who sows division and proudly displays ignorance and bigotry.

One reason for cynicism about government is that much of what government does for us is not visible. I wanted to make "government" and "taxes" real for my kids as they were growing up. When we drove by one of the dozens of free swimming pools in the city, we talked about how anyone with any level of income gets to cool off when it's 90 degrees out,

> AT ALMOST EVERY MONTHLY MEETING FOR HIS DEPARTMENT HEADS AND POLICY ADVISORS, MAYOR MENINO FIRMLY REMINDED US: OUR JOB IS TO IMPROVE THE LIVES OF ALL OF BOSTON'S CITIZENS, ESPECIALLY THOSE MOST VULNERABLE.

and a child of any means can learn to swim. To my kids I pointed out our tax dollars at work when we did pull-ups in a city park jungle gym, had our trash collected, or rode the subway, noting that the subway fares don't nearly cover what it costs to run the trains.

I think my kids got it. When they talked about a great sixth grade math teacher, they realized: we help pay for him. Or when a fire truck was racing to a blaze: we help make that happen with our taxes. Sometimes the conversations were more complex, as I remembered to add that there's no inherent incentive, beyond morality, for chemical companies to spend the money to safely dispose of toxic waste. Without government, who would monitor air quality and water safety? Making it real — what the role of government is and can be — makes it possible, in this case to understand that taxes are not inherently a waste, even if the tax code needs reinvention.

In this time of such divisiveness in our country and groups being pitted against one another, it's important we find ways to help our neighbors, colleagues, friends, and family members talk about the value of investing in removing barriers and name the misperception that we truly live in a meritocracy. A TEDx Talk by author-activist Chuck Collins, called "Taxing the Wealthy"[1] brought alive how we benefit from taxes and the existence of government, countering the myth that anyone is truly "self-made." Collins grew up in a wealthy family, heir to the Oscar Meyer fortune, raised with a trust fund. In his talk, he explains that many of his successes in life are due to doors opened and opportunities provided that others just don't have. Chuck speaks eloquently about the things that so-called "self-made men" conveniently ignore when they take sole credit for accomplishments: the taxes that pave the roads a company needs to bring their goods across state lines, the street lights that

IT'S SOMETHING TO SUCCESSFULLY SPRINT FROM THIRD BASE TO HOME PLATE, ADDING A RUN TO A TEAM'S TALLY; BUT THAT'S DIFFERENT THAN WHAT IT TAKES FOR SOMEONE STANDING AT THE PLATE WHO HAS TO HIT THE HOMER AND CROSS FOUR BASES BEFORE GETTING THE RUN. NOW IMAGINE THE PLAYER HAD NO ACCESS TO A BAT OR PLAYING FIELDS GROWING UP.

allow a company to function at night, the police force that makes a safe place for a company to operate, not to mention a plethora of tax breaks that lead some of our wealthiest corporations or individuals to pay no taxes at all. Self-made? Ha!

Collins's book, *Born on Third Base*, names a reality: It's something to successfully sprint from third base to home plate, adding a run to a team's tally; but that's different than what it takes for someone standing at the plate who has to hit the homer and cross four bases before getting the run. Now imagine the player had no access to a bat or playing fields or a neighborhood coach growing up.

It is important to make it real, what privilege looks like and what it looks like when people don't have it. I worked with my boss, the CEO of Thompson Island Outward Bound Education Center in the Boston Harbor, to pen his op-ed in the Boston Business Journal[2] in the spring of 2019, speaking from a similar perspective as Collins:

> *I benefited from — and took for granted — travel, camp, unpaid internships, trips to museums. The schools I attended had science fairs, robust arts and music programs, and well-equipped sports teams. In this country, by age 12, children from well-off families experience an average of 6,000 more hours of this kind of enrichment outside the classroom than their less advantaged peers… Against incredible odds, I see students in our island's education program strive mightily to become scholars, leaders, athletes, and then volunteer to give back to their community. In their presence, I realize that while I worked hard to get into college, it was not nearly as hard as these young people work. And when I made mistakes, cut corners, or got into trouble — as young people often do — the adults in my world would wink and send me on my way, the opposite of the fate faced by many of our students. Doors were held open for me, both when I deserved it and when I didn't. Those of us who had this kind of head start in life have a responsibility to open doors for others.*

Many of the people who have moved me the most in my travels through social justice terrain had to jump multiple hurdles to arrive at the plate to be able to swing the bat in the first place. One of the young adults who inspires me the most is J'Saun, who spent years studying with us at Thompson Island Outward Bound. He spoke at our annual gala a few years ago, to share his story.

Every year, from grades 6 through 12, J'Saun came to the island to learn science and team building, no matter what was going on at home and in his school. In his late teens, J'Saun came out to work and study for seven weeks each summer, heading to the island every day in the heat, to build new structures, maintain the fields, and later to mentor younger teens. Eventually I learned about his true passion, running. In the winter of 2017, we on staff found out that his four-person relay team had won the regionals in track, the first time in his urban public high school's history that any team would be going to the state championship! They won there, coming from behind. Now, how to afford to get to nationals? They created a GoFundMe page. In two days, after the page was posted, 92 people made contributions beginning as low as $5 each, to send the team to compete and represent Massachusetts. Now that's a home run for us all.

I was pleased to see that a 2013 *Boston Globe* interview[3] made it real how the country benefits from investing in our youth, including through our tax dollars. Harvard Graduate School of Education professor Todd Rose wrote that he dropped out of high school to take a $4.25 per hour job. He went on to overcome the hurdles that had limited his life, penning *Square Peg: My Story and What It Means for Raising Innovators, Visionaries, & Out-of-the-Box Thinkers*.

Now working to revamp our education system, in the interview, Todd Rose reflects on the help he received, noting that a free, public education is an essential component of the American dream, with an impact far beyond the students themselves: "Virologist Jonas Salk's parents immigrated and he went to the City College of New York, which doesn't charge tuition. We made that bet as a public: If you went to school on the taxpayer's dime, you could succeed. And then Jonas Salk cured polio and he gave that cure away. The impact of that one innovation changed the world. What if our cure for cancer is a Latina girl sitting in a crowded classroom in Oakland?"

Throughout *Chasing Social Justice* I have named shortcomings, including my own, in how we operate in the public and nonprofit sectors and in our political movements. I've suggested approaches that veer away from over-simplification and polarization:

- Become less ambivalent about ambivalence, reserving the right to learn continuously, and sometimes to change our mind. Doors open when we amp up the dialogue about complex issues which rightfully provoke ambivalence, and amp down diatribe.
- We must overtly name continued inequities in a country that holds itself up as the standard bearer for equality and opportunity. If we don't even name it, we surely won't fix it.
- Our social change efforts are most effective when we combine the best of human contact with emerging technologies.
- When we are building things — whether a coalition or the architecture of a young child's brain — it's more effective and efficient to do it right from the start than to hope we have the tools and funding to correct problems later on.
- We don't need to choose between, and only consider, top-down and bottom-up types of change; the most lasting movements are both and more: top-down, bottom up, and middle-out.

I have shared with you the approaches, concepts, and specifics that I believe lead us away from the dead-end questions that stymie our work, well-meaning but misguided queries such as:

- *How can we do more with less?* It is much more effective to be strategic, to develop our vision, before we limit our thinking. So change the question to: What it is we need to achieve, and what kind of investments would it take to get there?
- *Should women work?* Given the reality that women do and will work, and men too will work, it's time to stop complaining that we are behind other industrialized countries and instead to implement intelligent work-family policies, while we fight for all employees to work reasonable hours. (While this book is by no means focused on work/family issues, I point out this question as an example of how we need to be less insular: many assert this country is so advanced, and yet we lag far behind policy changes made in other places on earth.)
- *We built it, so why didn't they come?* Instead we must ask: How do we design our new project with the essential input and buy-in of our target audience, and how do we then make sure they know about it and make use of it?
- *What is* THE *answer?* Instead: What are the multiple, intersecting factors that need to change for us to solve this problem, and in what order should we tackle them?

Where can we make a difference?, I asked in the introduction, echoing the question posed by my friend's mother, Nancy.

Every summer, during the reunion with my college gang, I think about Nancy's challenge. The five of us from those days at Brown have been fortunate to stay close over the years and find our way to purposeful work. Jane is an ob-gyn, whose career has spanned research on HIV prevention for women in developing countries to studies on racial disparities in infant survival in the US. She helped scores of patients give birth, and then became a health care executive. Kate shares her passion for literature as an English teacher and administrator at an independent school in San Francisco. For much of her adult life she cared for her aging parents, diagnosed with separate diseases that sent them into hospitals and long-term care facilities. We watched in awe as our dear friend chose to use that experience to guide other people through the process of losing a parent to a slow, debilitating illness.

Our third friend, Arthur, has spent decades working with authors around the world to publish creative and diverse literature for children and young adults. He now runs his own publishing house. The fourth friend became a pediatrician: Cindy treats patients in an urban public hospital, often those struggling with the challenges that accompany poverty, while training our country's future doctors. And my story you have already heard.

At reunions over the years, our questions related to work have moved from which arena to operate in, to how do we keep on keeping on, avoiding burnout and cynicism. Three overlapping themes emerge: Connection, Balance, and Perspective.

NOTICE CONNECTION

When I stop to soak in the way people care for, take care of, and celebrate each other, I can't help but stay energized.

In the spring of 2018, Boston featured a month-long spell of rain, following the coldest winter on record. On one of the darkest days, I watched the way people connected across race and class — on the subway, in the elevator, in line at the grocery store. As in the middle of a snow-storm, when people turn out to shovel a neighbor's sidewalk, everyone had one thing in common — feeling wet and annoyed — and the sense of humor of strangers made a world of difference. Weather and children often bridge our divisions, don't they?

Riding up the elevator at a Boston business that month, I saw a dad grin at his son, who was maybe three years old: "Show me the button for floor 25." He yelped with pride when the little guy got it right. I looked around and everyone in the elevator — who had been speaking different languages, wearing clothes that ranged from a burqa to a tie-dyed bandana — stopped to high-five the kid. Connection. The shared joy of watching a child's mind expand.

SEEK BALANCE — FOR OURSELVES AND OTHERS

Daily life offers us opportunities to understand ongoing inequities and to re-inspire ourselves to do better.

In my mind, I can still see her collapse, as if in slow motion. In the middle of picking out groceries at the large supermarket, a woman fell. Her leg buckled, the basket of food on her arm flying everywhere, as she crashed to the floor. I thought she was having a seizure, the way she writhed.

It turned out her knee had dislocated. As she lay in excruciating pain, her leg twisted in a gruesome position nature never intended, what did this woman do? She reached into her purse, with most of the contents spilled out next to her, pulled out her cell phone, and proceeded to call work to say she couldn't come in! I could tell the person on the other end of the phone was actually arguing with her that she indeed had to come in. What struck me the most was that she not only balanced intense pain with making a phone call while lying on the linoleum floor, but she fluidly moved from English to Haitian Creole to French as she spoke to various people on the phone.

As I sat with her, she moaned, said she was worried both about getting to her job that night and to her second job the next day, Saturday. It sounded like one of her jobs was as a home health aide.

The cultural differences between us were stark. A reserved Haitian woman, she was obviously experiencing the kind of pain I had only endured during childbirth. While I would have been yelling my Jewish head off, she was mostly silent, squeezing the blood out of my hand. When the EMTs finally arrived and lifted her onto the stretcher, she kept crying out quietly, "Oh my God, oh my God, I am going to scream," as if it were the worst thing one could possibly do.

I had never seen someone able to manage so much while in pain — her young son who was with her, those phone calls. When I called a week later, having taken down her phone number, she was just getting out of the hospital. She commented quietly, resigned, that no one from her weekend job had called to see how she was doing.

So I think about balance. I have three kids (ages 17, 21, and 24 as

I write this), and I'm pretty clear that my primary legacy in life will be to provide a mix of support and challenge, guidance and freedom, limits and choices, to them. When they were younger and questioned a decision I made, to keep myself calm, I restated my motto: "My job is to keep you safe and healthy and to help you grow up to be a good person." It's a simplistic phrase, and not always possible to protect our kids like that, but the motto kept me focused — making it real — when they tested me.

When my kids were young, and I found myself missing them or feeling terribly strained, I would ask myself, "Am I going to end world hunger today?" I am not kidding, I honestly asked that. And when the answer was no, I decided it was okay to be late to a meeting or two; to make it to my son's basketball game, go for a run, or stop and visit a neighbor whose father had just died.

This troubles me, though, because there is inherent privilege in even talking about living a "balanced" life, certainly not an option open to the woman who fell in the grocery store. During the Massachusetts 2014 gubernatorial election, the two finalists disagreed about whether to support a ballot question for something called the Earned Sick Time initiative, with the victor opposing it (but fortunately, voters overwhelmingly approved it). During discussions on the question, I shook my head about the slow pace of change, and how short our collective memory can be.

LET'S NAME IT: IT STILL TAKES THE SPECTER OF AN INTERNATIONAL CRISIS, A PANDEMIC, FOR OUR COUNTRY TO CONSIDER SICK TIME AND OTHER LEAVE FOR EMPLOYEES WHO DON'T HAVE UNION PROTECTIONS AND WHO DO NOT WORK IN SENIOR POSITIONS.

I reflected again on sick time when fears of the coronavirus spread in early 2020, bringing analogies to when SARS emerged in 2003. Many people don't remember the swine flu (H1N1) emergency in 2009–2010. I was working in the mayor's office and watched with pride how our public health commissioner kept panic down in the city. One of the strongest messages was to stay home if sick, and to stay home for the duration of symptoms — seven days. We talked internally about how unrealistic this would be for most families, and it was then scaled back to a recommendation of four days at home following a fever.

To halt the frightening number of total-school closures during the swine flu epidemic, working parents were urged to break the unspoken tradition of providing a sick child with Tylenol and sending them on to school. But we also asked ourselves: How could a parent possibly do this — stay home or keep their child home for four days — if they had a job that provided no paid sick leave or, worse, penalized employees for being out?

So why does it take a new virus for us to revisit the lack of sick leave for employees in many American industries? Let's name it: it still takes the specter of an international crisis, a pandemic, for our country to consider sick time and other leave for employees who don't have union protections and who do not work in senior positions.

The Earned Sick Time bill introduced in the Massachusetts legislature not long after the swine flu scare called for smaller companies to offer five days of unpaid sick leave per year. Many companies, it turned out, according to a *Boston Globe* article,[4] were offering only one week annually of paid vacation and sick leave combined per year for employees in their first four years of work. The article compared sick leave policy in various states. It revealed that in Massachusetts, 36 percent of employers provided no paid sick leave to their workers, affecting 900,000 employees.

> BUT HOPE ISN'T FOOLISH. WE CAN BALANCE OPTIMISM AND REALISM, JUST AS WE CAN HANDLE MORE COMPLEXITY IN THIS COUNTRY'S DEBATES THAN WE HAVE ALLOWED OURSELVES TO DATE.

The piece included examples of parents who were threatened with the loss of their job if they stayed home with a sick child, parents who then had to beg the child's daycare provider to let the kid attend while sick, thus of course exposing other children to illness.

So one way to keep on keeping on is — for anyone privileged enough to have a shot at work/life balance — to indeed keep balance in our life, and continue to strive for the rights of all citizens to fair working conditions that allow individuals and families to thrive.

KEEP PERSPECTIVE WHILE WE KEEP UP THE PACE

Is the glass half empty or half full? Actually, it's always full — partly with water and partly with air! Seriously, though, some of my colleagues and friends have asked how I remain a glass-is-half-full gal, given the crazy world in which we live and the ways I've seen that close up: people dying of AIDS whose parents reject them; teenagers living in the foster care system and then sent off on their own with no support or resources; children entering kindergarten without books in their house, and without enough food for dinner, expected to keep up with their peers.

Yes, we are falling short on many fronts. Who would have guessed that in 2009, a group like the Tea Party would have taken hold in the US at all, let alone taken the Republican Party hostage, bringing it farther to the right? Numerous racially motivated murders in the past decade brought to the surface long-simmering pain and put truth to the lie that racism no longer exists. I am blown away that in the decade prior to the coronavirus Congress couldn't come together to extend unemployment benefits even in times of economic crisis, as tax-paying citizens — lifelong hard workers — demonstrated very clearly that they were pounding the pavement, and no jobs existed to feed their family. And many of us are still in shock that the country could elect someone like Donald Trump as president, given how much disdain he displayed towards those who are most vulnerable in our society. Of all his early efforts, the one that troubled me the most was creating an office dedicated solely to investigating crimes committed by immigrants, a callous disregard for reality and a cheap effort to play to his base and create scapegoats; in fact, native-born United States residents commit crime at about twice the rate of immigrants.[5]

Yes, we are falling short on many fronts, but perspective helps us keep up our pace. Let's not take for granted dramatic changes in recent decades. We've finally almost killed the cigarette industry when for decades their products merrily killed us. I don't take for granted progress made in our lifetimes or those of our parents: Birth control only became legal in 1960; interracial couples have only been able to marry since 1967; and no one would have guessed that in the short span from 2004 to 2015, the country would move from one state allowing same-sex marriage to the Supreme Court making marriage equality legal across the nation. The 2015 movie *Selma* reminded us that it was only 50 years ago that we passed the Voting Rights Act, clearing the basic hurdles that stopped Black people from voting. (And yet we must remain vigilant to voter suppression efforts around the country, especially after the Supreme Court gutted the Voting Rights Act in 2013.)

Much has changed, and is changing still, for the better, for the good. I don't take for granted that our kids are growing up automatically recycling; I remember the time in City Hall only 12 years ago when we experimented with single-stream recycling (tossing together glass, newspaper, plastic) to make it more doable, and then we moved on to create bike lanes. Most bike lanes didn't exist until a decade ago.

President Obama was on to something when he chose the title *Audacity of Hope* for his second book. It does take something powerful in us, something deep, to maintain hope in the face of so many defeats here and around the world — the obstacles to fairness and justice, our inability to meet basic human needs on a planet with an embarrassment of riches. But hope isn't foolish. We can balance optimism and realism, just as we can handle more complexity in this country's debates than we have allowed ourselves to date. For me, this means slowing down at times to take note of our progress; finding balance, as we keep perspective; and never ceasing the work, since lives are still at stake, whether the cause be poverty, violence, or the impact of dreams deferred.

Here you have read my lessons learned and my reflections from three decades of traveling a path toward social justice. How would I capture in one vibrant image these spectacular views from my journey? In the picture of glorious rising mountains and volcanic-sized holes, I see people falling down . . . and people moving swiftly to help others up.

Todd Rose's reminder about Jonas Salk and his gift to us all of a polio vaccine, and Todd's reflection about the Latina girl who might be our next best chance, brought to mind a three-year-old Chinese boy I met while working in City Hall. I was staffing one of Mayor Menino's Countdown to Kindergarten events, where the little boy proudly sported his bright yellow "I'm Going to Kindergarten" T-shirt. Boston kindergarten starts as young as age three for a child with special needs, and every entering kindergartner receives the free shirt from the schools as an admission ticket to local events, many held in the neighborhood libraries.

Hearing that I represented the mayor, the boy's mom came over and told me a bit about their family's struggle. She then introduced little Kahn to me. He said hello out loud in English and Chinese, while making the matching motion in American Sign Language.

Seeing the device in his ear that indicated a cochlear implant, I smiled as his mother proudly announced, "He speaks three languages!" The staff at Early Intervention had helped her as soon as he was diagnosed as deaf right after birth, and the specialists in the Boston schools were assisting with the transition from a community program into kindergarten. This spunky, confident little boy, born to a mom with limited income, had benefited from a resilient family, combined with publicly funded services. Many people came together to get him off to the right start, leveling his sandbox.

Making that kind of investment in our fellow citizens fulfills the American dream of equal opportunity, and it expands the numbers of people who can bring their best to our society.

Who will we help up? Who will then go on to reach a hand back to someone else?

If we make their classroom less crowded, continuing to cut doors and windows into the walls surrounding their lives, perhaps Kahn and that girl

> WE CAN ENSURE THAT THE STUNNING LANDSCAPES THROUGHOUT THIS PLANET ENDURE AND THAT HUMANITY GROWS THE MUSCLES OF TENACITY AND COMPASSION.

from Oakland will team up to cure cancer. Maybe they will grow up to lead our country toward a new way to partner with other nations to prevent war. Or ensure that no child around the world goes without clean water and widely available immunizations. Or identify solutions to climate change.

We can pave a path for and with our fellow citizens, lowering the highest hurdles, filling the deepest potholes. We can rise together. We can prevent devastating war and natural disasters brought about from unfettered climate change. We can ensure that the stunning landscapes throughout this planet endure and that humanity grows the muscles of tenacity and compassion. We can tackle deep cultural divisions that keep us from bringing to the table our best ideas for solving our toughest challenges. Each of us, and together all of us, can pursue and embrace social justice.

AFTERWORD

As this first edition of *Chasing Social Justice* goes to print and e-book in April of 2020, COVID-19 is peaking in parts of the United States and other countries. What happens on the other side of the apex is unclear. What we will truly learn from the pandemic — in terms of epidemiology, public health, economics, and social justice — is even more unclear.

I have been turning to the concepts in *Chasing* to help me think through my own next steps, from which efforts to support with my charitable donations to how I should focus my time.

While I am tempted to share my analysis and my hopes, as I note throughout the book, the kinds of questions we ask are often more important than offering a particular opinion or solution. In a few pages you'll see my suggested questions for using the book in graduate or undergrad courses, or in discussion groups, looking at a wide range of justice issues. In terms of COVID-19, I would add:

ON NAMING AND THE POWER OF OUR WORDS:
- Many agreed that it was crucial not to call this "the Wuhan virus" or "the Chinese virus." What are your thoughts on that? Looking back at how other viruses have been named (from Zika to SARS to HIV), how were those decisions made and what were the implications?
- Was "social distancing" the right term? Why and why not?

ON KEEPING IT REAL AND THE IMPACT OF "WHAT DOES IT LOOK LIKE":
- When and how did social distancing become the norm versus something people resisted — what shifts in communication and what tools did you see that worked to help people (and groups of people, and individual states or countries) start to employ social distancing?
- Why did it take so long for it to become clear that people on the front lines (health professionals, first responders, people driving our buses, cleaning our hospitals, selling groceries) did not have the protective gear they needed to do their jobs without potentially getting themselves and their families sick?

ON POWER

- How did people in traditional positions of power — including elected officials, health professionals, business leaders, and others — use that power to advance or hamper public health measures, here or in other countries?
- Did you notice any individuals or groups that you might normally not have thought of as having power (or who themselves might not have thought they had power) who made a difference in the pandemic?
- What did you do with your own power during the pandemic?

ON THE HUMAN CONNECTION:

- In what ways were connections strengthened and weakened during the pandemic, thinking more deeply than just that we stood farther apart and that many people learned to do video calls?
- How can we build on the successful efforts to maintain and deepen relationships during the shutdown, in order to further our work after the pandemic?

ON MARKETING AND MEDIA:

- Was it okay, in your opinion, that the 2020 election and many other newsworthy topics were rarely covered during the pandemic? If not, how might we have kept various issues in the forefront of media attention, such as what was happening to children and families separated by recent immigrant regulations?
- Many people noted that not nearly enough was done to ensure that the CARES act funds for the Paycheck Protection Plan could reach all the relevant small businesses and nonprofits, not just those in the know. What should have been done differently?
- What media coverage did you see that was effective in raising justice aspects of the virus, such as the disproportionate impact on people of color and people without paid sick leave?

ON AMBIVALENCE:

- Where did you come up against ambivalence of your own during the pandemic?

- What examples did you see of other people wrestling with ambivalence and then getting to the other side?
- When we look back in years to come, will we have made the right decisions about when to loosen the restrictions on social distancing and re-open businesses?

ON THAT ANGEL IN THE DETAILS:

- How did meetings or coalitions improve or deteriorate during the pandemic? Are there takeaways from how people and organizations and businesses managed meetings and coalitions that will help us moving forward?

ON PREVENTION (THAT CONCEPT OF STARTING WITH THE SANDBOX):

- In addition to knowing that our country's leaders should have responded more aggressively before the virus took hold, are there lessons we can take away from the pandemic that will help the country better prioritize prevention in a policy arena that matters to you?

DISCUSSION QUESTIONS

INTRODUCTION: WHERE CAN WE MAKE A DIFFERENCE?

- What is your definition of social justice?
- When did you first learn about injustice? Has your concept of justice and injustice changed since then?
- How would you describe the different ways to be involved in advancing justice?

CHAPTER 1: WHAT'S IN A NAME?

- The author argues that we can't solve problems we are not naming. What is one social justice issue you think is not being talked about enough?
- What did you think and what did you feel when you read the sections about education inequities? Is this a problem we can resolve?
- What did you think of the story where a group of AIDS activists confronted a progressive gay newspaper staff about not covering the epidemic? When is it important to put effort towards people who are often allies but may not be doing enough, versus against those in higher level positions of power?

CHAPTER 2: KEEPING IT REAL

- How can a person with privilege(s) use it to advance justice? Where might the challenges lie?
- In this chapter, the author uses many examples that are not taken from social justice, but from daily life. Is this effective or distracting? Share an area in your life/work where it might make a difference to pose the question "What does that look like?"

CHAPTER 3: POWER

- Do you agree with the author that everyone has power and can identify and use it, or does that minimize the experience of people who are struggling mightily?
- If you are not someone who has worked in government, did reading the author's stories in this chapter (and other chapters) impact your perspective on government and government employees?
- What was your reaction to the author's examples of how she used her power in various situations (from the group home to the mayor's office to the subway)? Did the examples seem like the right use of power to you? What might you have done differently in those situations?
- Are there examples where you have seen people in formal positions of power wield it appropriately and avoid operating in a bubble, making sure to stay informed and to have the people around them continue to challenge them?

CHAPTER 4: THE HUMAN CONNECTION

- Do you think the author is right that the existence of technology has at times led to activists forgetting to make direct human contact, to their detriment?
- Can you name an example of an organization or campaign using traditional outreach methods combined with effective use of technology?
- In your own experience, when have you seen in-person communication make a difference in terms of outcome or impact?
- Human connections are of course affected by prejudices, social barriers, and political differences, among other factors. How do you navigate making contact with people who have a different social status or a different level of power from you?

CHAPTER 5: TO MARKET, TO MARKET

- Does the focus of this chapter — that a failure to market is a top mistake in nonprofit and justice work — reflect your experience? Do you agree with the author's assertion that "there is no conflict between doing good work and telling the story"?
- What examples have you seen of effective marketing making a difference for a nonprofit or for social justice work?

CHAPTER 6: WORD FIND

- This chapter features many examples of words to use and words to avoid. Did the examples of wording to shift resonate with you, or did some seem unnecessary?
- What words have you moved away from in your work, and what words have you in turn begun to use? Have you seen changed word choices make a difference in your work?
- What do you think of the author's assertion that the term "gun control" is part of the reason the movement to end gun violence is stalling?
- One might argue that it isn't the words used but how one uses words that matters. For example, President Trump used a wide range of words in new ways (such as "fake news"), but his forte seemed to be simply stating and re-stating a subjective or untrue concept (such as all media that criticized his policies was simply biased against him) and sometimes stating and re-stating an outright falsehood (that the crowd at his inauguration was the largest ever, or that he won by a landslide) until it took hold. During the COVID-19 pandemic, after insisting the virus was not a risk in the U.S., he outright lied that he had ever downplayed the threat, once the virus spread, asserting that he was a pro-active leader at all times. What are

your thoughts about how words are currently used? Would you be willing to use incorrect statements or outright lies to advance a cause you believe in?

CHAPTER 7: MEDIA MATTERS

- What forms of media do you use to remain informed? Have you found ways to avoid being in a self-reinforcing bubble? Have you found sources that provide you with viewpoints you might not have thought of or with which you might disagree?
- Have you found any successful ways to encourage people who think differently from you to question what they are reading or watching or listening to?
- In your work or in organizations you support, what are examples of using existing media well and also of creating your own media?

CHAPTER 8: AMBIVALENCE

- Can you name issues on which your stance has changed as a result of allowing yourself to question an original stance and take in new information?
- Are there issues about which you are currently ambivalent — where you might have a clear stance on how you would vote, for example, but some aspects of the issue are still weighing on you?

CHAPTER 9: THE ANGEL'S IN THE DETAILS

- Share an example of a crucial meeting that was ineffective because the basics weren't addressed.
- Are there other steps you have seen or used yourself that ensure effective meetings and successful coalitions?
- The author notes that technology can be a boon (allowing

people to meet across the world) or a bust (everyone in an important meeting is on their phones, distracted by other business). How do you manage this in your work?

CHAPTER 10: LEVELING THE SANDBOX
- If you are not involved in early childhood work, did you find this chapter useful and the concepts applicable? If so, how so?
- How have you seen a commitment to prevention (versus intervention and remediation) make a difference in an organization or a movement?
- As you read the author's examples of how she applied the lessons in Chasing Social Justice (CSJ) to her work on early childhood issues, did you see applications of the CSJ ideas that would move your work forward?

CONCLUSION: HOW DO WE KEEP ON KEEPING ON?
- How do you keep on keeping on?
- The author lists four questions as examples of ones that hold us back. Are there other common questions that polarize and simplify?

OVERALL DISCUSSION QUESTIONS:
- The author identifies herself as white and having grown up primarily middle class, with some stages of financial insecurity. Are there places where her own biases or privilege come through that she is not seeing? Are there times you have caught yourself with an implicit or unconscious bias?
- What information did you find most helpful in the book? What, if anything, was surprising or new?
- Of the principles explored in the book, which ones seem

most relevant to your work? How might you incorporate them in your efforts to chase social justice? Are there other key lessons you have learned from being involved in or observing social justice work?

- The author was aiming to make a sometimes hefty and heady subject — social justice and social policy — accessible and interesting, with a combination of personal perspective and factual information. Did she succeed?

APPRECIATIONS

First, thank you to Leah, Aiden and Eleanor. You are often my best teachers.

Every stage of my work has provided opportunities to learn from more people than I can list. In addition to those named within the text, and all of my current Outward Bound colleagues, I thank these leaders, colleagues, and mentors:

Abe Rybeck

Alexandra Elizabeth

Alyce Lee

Amika Kemmler Ernst

Amy O'Leary

Analisa Nena

Anand Vaishnav

Anita Rossien

Angela Menino

Ann Collins

Annie Fischer

Arlene Fortunato

Arlene Isaacson

Arthur Pearson

Barbara Berke

Barbara Ferrer

Beth Greenberg Jones

Bill Elcock

Bill Margolin

Blanca Valentin

Bob Sege

Bob Van Meter

Bob Wadsworth

Brian Corr

Carolyn O'Brien

Casel Walker

Cassandra Baxter

Cheng Imm Tan

Cherie Craft

Cheryl Schaffer

Chris Horan

Chris Wittke

Clare Reilly

Corey Zimmerman

Daria Smith

David Passafaro

David Wilson

Deborah Allen

Deborah Dickerson

Denise Snyder

Dennis DiMarzio

Dewaine Osman

Diane Joyce

Dina Siegal

Doris Roach

Dot Joyce

Doug Baird

Ed Davis

Eileen Costello

Elaine Zecher

Elizabeth Pauley

Ed Davis

Enrico Mezzacappa
Gary Sandison
Ginny Zanger
Gordon Gottlieb
Harold Dufour
Harold Sparrow
Harry Collings
Harry Smith
Heavenly Mitchell
Helen Ardine
Helen Dajer
Hirokazu Yoshikawa
Howard Leibowitz
Hung Wei Speicher
Jack Shonkoff
Jack Vondras
Jacquelyn Goddard
Jason Sachs
Javier Parra
Jeff Hayward
Jeff Sanchez
Jeri Robinson
Jerry Mogul
Jill Epstein
John Barros
John Connolly
John Hogan
John Riordan
Jon Chilingerian
Jonah Pesner
Joy Cochran
Joy Oliver
Juanita Wade
Julia Ojeda
Kate Bennett

Kate Weldon LeBlanc
Kathleen Colby
Kathleen Traphagen
Katie Britton
Kim Willingham
Klare Shaw
Lainy Fersh
Larry Kessler
Laura Perille
Leslie Bos
Linda Kowalcky
Liz Page
Liz Walczak
Liz Walker
Loie Hayes
Lourdes Sariol
Lydia Agro
Lyn Freundlich
Marcos Bistecas-Cocoves
Margaret Blood
Marie St. Fleur
Marinell Rousmaniere
Marta Rosa
Martha Pierce
Marty Walsh
Matt LiPuma
Matthew Soffer
Max Fripp
May Vaughn
Melanie Adler
MH Nsangou
Mia Alvarado
Michael Kelley
Mike Kineavy
Mike Ross

Mindy Fried

Mireille Louis

Nancy Marks

Nancy Osman

Natasha Vianna

Pat Xavier

Patty Leary-Gomez

Peg Sprague

Peter Welsh

Paul Grogan

Rachel Blumberg

Rachel Goodman

Rachel Weinstein

Randal Rucker

Ray Hammond

Rick Weissbourd

Rob Consalvo

Robert Lewis Jr.

Robyn Ochs

Roland Tang

Ronne Friedman

Ross Wilson

Sacha Pfeiffer

Sally Fogerty

Sandi Henriquez

Sandy Sachs

Sara Stone

Seth Gitell

Shari Nethersole

Sister Helen Sullivan

Stephanie Poggi

Steve Gag

Sue Hyde

Sue Naimark

Susan Tracy

Theresa Lynn

Tim Garvin

Tom Tinlan

Valora Washington

Vicki Gabriner

Wayne Ysaguirre

Zamawa Arenas

It takes a village! My heartfelt thanks to those who helped make the book itself possible:

- *Editors:* Beth Wright — you changed the whole way I thought about the personal side of the book and provided a level of discipline that transformed the work; Lise Stern — you rearranged chapters and concepts in a way that helped me pull it all together; and Beth Wallace — your initial editing made my thinking more sophisticated and clear.
- *Readers of the very first draft, years ago* — you all were rock stars to wade through that meandering manuscript! Natasha Vianna, Adam Frost, Genessa Trietsch, David Trietsch, Sarah Pace

- *Additional book advisors and supporters:* Shelley Mains, Mike Sherman, Jeff Sherman, Alex Sherman, Tom Siegel
- *Fact checker:* Elias Battles
- *Proofreader:* Liz Pease
- *Inside design & production:* Jenifer Snow Design
- *E-book production:* Alexsis Banales with Book Bloks
- *Cover design:* Okomota/The Design Lab

NOTES

CHAPTER 1

1. Matthew M. Chingos and Grover J. Russ Whitehurst, "Class Size: What Research Says and What it Means for State Policy." *Brookings Institute,* May 11, 2011, https://www.brookings.edu/research/class-size-what-research-says-and-what-it-means-for-state-policy/.

2. Matt O'Brien, "Poor kids who do everything right don't do better than rich kids who do everything wrong," *The Washington Post,* October 18, 2014, https://www.washingtonpost.com/news/wonk/wp/2014/10/18/poor-kids-who-do-everything-right-dont-do-better-than-rich-kids-who-do-everything-wrong/.

3. "The 6,000 Hour Learning Gap," ExpandED Schools, October 13, 2013, https://www.expandedschools.org/policy-documents/6000-hour-learning-gap#sthash.QsffhGWW.M2ziVfBU.dpbs.

4. "Anatomy of a 6,000-hour deficit," *Hechinger Ed* (blog), The Hechinger Report, November 4, 2013, http://hechingered.org/content/anatomy-of-a-6000-hour-deficit_6457/.

5. "Can I Borrow Your Weedwhacker? My Experience with Parent Engagement," *On the Level* (blog), September 5, 2016, https://lauriesherman.wixsite.com/otl-blog/single-post/2016/08/25/Can-I-Borrow-Your-Weedwhacker-My-Experience-with-Parent-Engagement.

6. James Vaznis, "Struggling Brockton schools may sue the state," *The Boston Globe,* March 17, 2018, https://www.bostonglobe.com/metro/2018/03/17/with-schools-struggling-brockton-considers-suing-state/dX0AKkDZS2nEZWly13PFOI/story.html.

7. Leigh Hofheimer, "Rape Prevention Tips," *Can You Relate?* (blog), May 24, 2011, https://canyourelate.org/2011/05/24/rape-prevention-tips/.

CHAPTER 6

1. "Firearm Access is a Risk Factor for Suicide," Harvard School of Public Health, 2016, https://www.hsph.harvard.edu/means-matter/means-matter/risk/.

2. "People First Language," Texas Council for Developmental

Disabilities, n.d., accessed March 6, 2020, https://tcdd.texas.gov/re-sources/people-first-language/#people.

CHAPTER 7

1. "Matt Confesses: Where the Hell is Matt? Video an 'Elaborate Hoax,'" YouTube, January 2, 2009, https://www.youtube.com/watch?v=ogcq-FaNbah4.
2. Naval Institute Staff, "Key Dates in U.S. Military LGBT History," March 26, 2018, https://www.navalhistory.org/2018/03/26/key-dates-in-u-s-military-lgbt-policy.
3. Yvonne Abraham," Learning to Love," The Boston Globe, September 2, 2007, http://archive.boston.com/news/local/articles/2007/09/02/learning_to_love/.

CHAPTER 8

1. "New CDC Report: STDs Continue to Rise in the U.S.," Centers for Disease Control and Prevention, October 8, 2019, https://www.cdc.gov/nchhstp/newsroom/2019/2018-STD-surveillance-report-press-release.html.
2. Rachel L. Swarns, "The Science Behind 'They All Look Alike to Me,'" The New York Times, September 20, 2015, https://www.nytimes.com/2015/09/20/nyregion/the-science-behind-they-all-look-alike-to-me.html.
3. Sarah Birnbaum, "Anti-Muslim Backlash Missing From Marathon Bombing Aftermath," WGBH, April 17, 2014, https://www.wgbh.org/news/post/anti-muslim-backlash-missing-marathon-bombing-aftermath.

CHAPTER 10

1. https://heckmanequation.org/

CONCLUSION

1. Chuck Collins, "Taxing the Wealthy," Tedx Talk, November 15, 2011, https://www.youtube.com/watch?v=1sgaDbg2RLE.
2. Arthur Pearson, "Viewpoint: Opening doors for young people is

moral, educational imperative," April 30, 2019, *Boston Business Journal,* https://www.bizjournals.com/boston/news/2019/04/29/view-point-opening-doors-for-young-people-is-moral.html.

3. Francie Latour, "Dropout at Harvard," *The Boston Globe*, March 31, 2013, https://c.o0bg.com/ideas/2013/03/30/dropout-harvard/3JEYV7sdiHzhlFNOapHSuO/story.html?p1=AMP_Recirculation_Pos3.

4. Megan Woolhouse, "Calls rising for paid sick days," *Boston Globe*, April 15, 2013

5. Christopher Ingraham, "Two charts demolish the notion that immigrants here illegally commit more crime," *The Washington Post,* June 19, 2018, https://www.washingtonpost.com/news/wonk/wp/2018/06/19/two-charts-demolish-the-notion-that-immigrants-here-illegally-commit-more-crime/.

**EMAIL YOUR FEEDBACK TO IMPROVE FUTURE EDITIONS
OF *CHASING SOCIAL JUSTICE***

Laurie@ChasingSocialJustice.com

ABOUT THE AUTHOR

Over the past three decades, Laurie Sherman has worked in public health, educational equity, neighborhood organizing, and human rights. For 17 of those years, she served as a policy advisor for Tom Menino, Boston's longest-serving mayor. While working for Mayor Menino, Laurie spearheaded the creation of the city's plan to prevent the academic achievement gap in the next generation of students. She is currently the executive vice president at Thompson Island Outward Bound Education Center in the Boston Harbor.

Laurie holds a Master's degree in Management and Social Policy from Brandeis University's Heller Graduate School and an undergraduate degree from Brown.

The proud parent of three young adults, she lives in Brookline, MA with her husband Jim.

Made in the USA
Middletown, DE
18 July 2020